BIBLE PROPHECY UNDER SIEGE

RON RHODES

HARVEST PROPHECY
AN IMPRINT OF HARVEST HOUSE PUBLISHERS

Scripture versions used in this book are listed at the back of the book.

Cover design by Bryce Williamson

Cover image © benoitb / Getty Images

Interior design by KUHN Design Group

For bulk, special sales, or ministry purchases, please call 1-800-547-8979.
Email: Customerservice@hhpbooks.com

This logo is a federally registered trademark of the Hawkins Children's LLC. Harvest House
Publishers, Inc., is the exclusive licensee of this trademark.

Bible Prophecy Under Siege
Copyright © 2024 by Ron Rhodes
Published by Harvest House Publishers
Eugene, Oregon 97408
www.harvesthousepublishers.com

ISBN 978-0-7369-8806-3 (pbk)
ISBN 978-0-7369-8807-0 (eBook)

Library of Congress Control Number: 2023938656

Printed in the United States of America

23 24 25 26 27 28 29 30 31 32 / VP / 10 9 8 7 6 5 4 3 2 1

*To all my Christian friends who are committed
to "rightly handling the word of truth"*

ACKNOWLEDGMENTS

Drs. John F. Walvoord, J. Dwight Pentecost, and Charles C. Ryrie were among my mentors at Dallas Theological Seminary in the 1980s. All three are now enjoying heavenly glory. The insightful teachings of these men played a significant role in shaping my views on Bible prophecy. Only eternity will reveal how many people they have blessed through their decades of teaching, preaching, and writing.

Words are inadequate to describe the blessing my wife Kerri has been to me through the decades. She is an "excellent wife" who is "far more precious than jewels" (Proverbs 31:10). She has consistently and faithfully stood by me and my work, and I could not have engaged in this life of ministry without her.

I truly appreciate my ongoing relationship with the fine team assembled at Harvest House Publishers—especially Bob Hawkins Jr. and Steve Miller. It is always a joy to work with Christians committed to spreading God's truth.

Most of all, I express profound appreciation to our Lord Jesus Christ, who will one day come again as the "King of kings and Lord of lords," and whose "eyes are like a flame of fire," and upon whose head "are many diadems" (Revelation 19:16, 12). Jesus motivates *all* my writing and ministry.

Come soon, Lord!

CONTENTS

INTRODUCTION:

BIBLE PROPHECY UNDER SIEGE

Y ou dummy!"

This barb came in an email from a rather feisty posttribulationist* who seemed to take pleasure at shooting down pretribulationists.

"The pretribulational rapture is heretical and speculative."

Another email from another posttribulationist.

"You pretribulationists barely understand the 'First Principles' of the Word of God."

Yet another email.

---

* *Posttribulationism* says the rapture will occur after the tribulation period; *pretribulationism* says it will occur before the tribulation period; *midtribulationism* says it will occur at the midpoint of the tribulation period.

"Pretribs* suffer from the pathology of 'escapism.' They are 'cowards'—afraid to go through the tribulation period."

Yet another email.

"If you teach people there is a rapture you might as well just worship Satan. That doctrine causes more harm than any demon."

A Facebook post.

A prominent midtribulationist wrote an article claiming that pre-tribulationism has a satanic origin—from a demon-possessed girl.

Another critic said in an article that pretribs have a "weak view of Scripture" and a "warped understanding of prophecy."

A preterist wrote that pretribulationism is "a deviation" and "a danger." It "has no validation in the Scriptures."

I'm beginning to resonate with the words of the psalmist: "O LORD, how many are my foes! Many are rising against me" (Psalm 3:1).

A JOURNEY BACK TO YESTERYEAR

In the late 1970s and early 1980s, I got both a master's degree and a doctoral degree from Dallas Theological Seminary. My primary prophecy mentor was the late Dr. John F. Walvoord. Those were good years!

Dr. Walvoord gave me some advice that has stuck with me through the decades: "Anyone who says their position on Bible prophecy has

---

* *Pretrib* is short for pretribulationist, while *posttrib* is short for posttribulationist.

no theological problems has not studied the issue carefully. While some positions have fewer problems than others, *they all have some problems."*

Like Walvoord, I believe pretribulationism has the fewest difficulties when compared to midtribulationism, posttribulationism, the pre-wrath view, the partial rapture view, and the preterist view. *(If you are unfamiliar with some of these terms, do not be concerned. I'll define them as we go along.)*

Following seminary, in the late 1980s, apologist Walter Martin hired me to work at the Christian Research Institute in Southern California. Before hiring me, he called me into his office, and we spent a good hour or more discussing theological issues. He wanted to assess our overall theological compatibility.

We did not see eye to eye on some aspects of prophecy. Walter believed in the posttribulational view of the rapture—he was convinced it would occur *after* the seven-year tribulation period. I hold to the pretribulational view—I believe the rapture will *precede* the tribulation period. There was plenty to talk about in that meeting. We went back and forth like ping-pong balls on all this. But we did so with kindness and respect.

After we finished our theological discussion, Walter got up from behind his desk and gave me one of those big bear hugs he was famous for. With great enthusiasm, he asked me to join the team at the Christian Research Institute (CRI). He felt our theological agreements far outweighed any disagreements, and that areas of dispute were on nonessential matters. *We could simply agree to disagree in an agreeable way on the finer points of Bible prophecy.* This was especially easy to do because we agreed on the big picture of Bible prophecy—we both agreed there would be a rapture, a second coming, a judgment, heaven for the saved, and hell for the unsaved. We just disagreed on the *timing* of the rapture.

After joining the team at CRI, I became heavily involved in the publications department. I hadn't been there long before Walter—the host of the national *Bible Answer Man* radio broadcast—exited earthly life and entered his heavenly home. Soon after, I became heavily involved in the broadcast department, regularly appearing on the *Bible Answer Man* broadcast. Over the next eight years, I answered an endless flow of questions on this live (and *lively*) daily national radio broadcast.

As I reflect on those years, I remember they were challenging because I was the only pretrib on staff. The other researchers were posttribs—although a few defined themselves with the well-worn cliché "pan-tribs," who believe it will all pan out in the end. We all coexisted quite nicely. Even though my associates were mainly Reformed in their theological outlook—and even though we got into some fierce debates on live national radio on prophecy—our relationships remained characterized by kindness and respect. I appreciate that about my time at CRI. Those years taught me it is possible to disagree on Bible prophecy without resorting to vitriol.

After serving at CRI for nearly a decade, it was time to move on. My parents and my wife's parents lived in Texas, and because of their rapidly advancing old age, they were experiencing some rather significant health challenges. As hard as the decision was, my wife and I both felt the need to leave the sunny west coast of California (where CRI was located at the time) and move to Texas to be nearer to our parents. An added benefit to our relocation was that our kids could spend more time with our parents in their final years. Looking back in hindsight, our relocation turned out to be wise.

FAST-FORWARD TO THE PRESENT DAY

Today, Bible prophecy is *under siege*. There are atheists, secular humanists, liberal Christian theologians, posttribulationists, midtribulationists, preterists, and many others who are launching vitriolic attacks—particularly against pretribulationism. The widespread acceptance of the pretrib view—the majority view by a huge margin—has brought out the critics in full force. Throughout the chapters in this book, I will give plenty of examples of these criticisms and how pretribs can respond biblically.

I receive a lot of emails from people who have read my books. The overwhelming majority of emails are from thoughtful Christians—most of them pretribulationists—who want to express thanks for one or another of my books. I so appreciate these many wonderful emails. They put wind in my sails!

Other emails are from Christians seeking answers to current theological attacks against pretribulationism. *(I'm always happy to help.)* Still other emails are from Christians seeking to convert me to posttribulationism or preterism. *(None have succeeded!)* It is unfortunate that some in this latter category of emails have used the word *heresy* in association with pretribulationism. To be fair, I am aware of at least some pretribs who have charged posttribs as being heretics. The charges are flying both ways. But pretribulationism is the larger target because it is much more popular than the other positions.

Some emails I have received are from unbelievers who spontaneously bought one of my books in a bookstore because the topic looked interesting to them. Some say they grew up in a Christian home but have since defected from Christianity and no longer believe in the "foolishness" of Bible prophecy.

Other emails come from former pretribs who are now posttribs or preterists. Such folks tell me they were formerly fooled by the "deception" of pretribulationism. Many of these folks seem extremely harsh in their rejection of pretribulationism. Some express bitter sarcasm.

Still other emails take a condescending approach, declaring that educated people who have studied the issue do not believe in pretribulationism. I am informed that we pretribs are apparently unaware of the severe problems with our view—both historical and theological.

My friends, it is time for me to respond. Truth be told, I wish I could write a five-volume response, with each volume weighing in at 500 pages. I honestly believe I could fill 2,500 pages in response to the critics! But the publisher would never go for it—and it would be far too expensive! I find myself in the same predicament so many authors face: *There is so much to say and so few pages to say it.* This means I must be highly selective in my approach and answer only the most pressing issues that will best help my readers. Also, please keep in mind that I write for the average Christian. I have tried to avoid complex academic argumentation.

Here is my promise to you: Even though some articles and books against pretribs are disrespectful and condescending, I will not respond in kind in this book. I intend to keep the discussion civil. I will focus my attention on Scripture, and, in some cases, history. My goal is to generate more *light* than *heat*. In areas where we disagree, I will seek to *agree to disagree in an agreeable way*—even if my critics choose not to do this. As an ambassador of Christ (2 Corinthians 5:20), it is not just *what* I say that is important, but *how* I say it as well.

If you are a pretribulationist, I believe you will be encouraged in reading this book and absorbing the biblical truths within it. Your commitment to pretribulationism will be strengthened, and your excitement about the coming rapture will be renewed.

I urge you to read this book in its entirety first. You can then keep the book on a nearby shelf to reference it as needed as the prophecy debates continue. I hope and pray that this book will serve as a source of prophetic strength for you in the years to come.

Through it all, remember that the day of your redemption draws near. Every day that passes brings the rapture one day closer. Indeed, "salvation is nearer to us now than when we first believed" (Romans 13:11). *Maranatha!*

1

BIBLE PROPHECY UNDER FIRE

I was once invited to speak on prophecy at a church affiliated with a theologically liberal denomination. I was initially hesitant to speak there. In my mind's eye, I could see myself (a theological conservative) being booed off the stage by a bunch of theological liberals. But then, I thought, these people really need to hear the truth. So, I accepted the invitation. I promptly prepared four messages on the highlights of Bible prophecy—one for Friday night, two for Saturday, and one for Sunday morning. I booked my flight and off I went.

Upon arriving at the church, I discovered—much to my surprise—that even though it was affiliated with a theologically liberal denomination, it was not itself a liberal church. These folks were hungry for the Word of God. The church's pastor informed me: "Our denomination's curriculum materials don't have anything on Bible prophecy. Not anything at all. *Not even an honorary mention!* We've heard plenty of claims from folks in our denomination about why we shouldn't bother with prophecy. But we think differently at this church. We are keen to learn the truth, not an edited version of the truth. That's why we invited you. We want to understand what the Bible really teaches about prophecy."

I cannot begin to tell you how much I enjoyed teaching these folks who were so hungry for God's Word. I not only taught four sessions, but stayed late after each one, answering an endless flow of questions about prophecy.

Some questions I answered at this church involved claims *against* prophecy, some of which had been voiced by leaders within the liberal denomination. In what follows, I will address these claims and other common claims against prophecy. Since Scripture calls us always to be prepared with an answer (1 Peter 3:15), it is essential to know these claims and how to respond to them.

• • •

Some critics claim the Bible does not provide an explicit timeline concerning future events. So, we really can't be sure about the order of end-times events.

While it is true that the Bible does not provide us with an explicit timeline, there are many chronological clues scattered throughout end-times prophecies in the Bible that enable us to discern the order of end-times events. Please allow me to present a few illustrations from Scripture:

1. We discover a contextual outline of John's prophetic book in Revelation 1:19. The Lord instructs John: "Write therefore the things that you have seen, those that are and those that are to take place after this." The "things that you have seen" is a reference to Revelation 1, where we find a description of Jesus in His present majestic glory and an introduction to the book of Revelation. The things "that are" relate to the then-present circumstances of the seven churches of Asia Minor recorded in Revelation 2 and 3. John directed his book to these seven churches. The things "that are to take place after this" refer to futuristic prophecy of the tribulation period, the second

coming, the millennial kingdom, the great white throne judgment, and the eternal state described in Revelation 6 through 22. This outline is a great aid to a proper understanding of the chronology of the book of Revelation.

2. A specific example from Revelation relates to how Satan will be bound for the duration of Christ's future 1,000-year millennial kingdom. There are chronological clues in the book of Revelation that confirm this for us. Notice the words I've italicized in the following passage: "I saw an angel coming down from heaven, holding in his hand the key to the bottomless pit and a great chain. And he seized the dragon, that ancient serpent, who is the devil and Satan, and *bound him for a thousand years*, and threw him into the pit, and shut it and sealed it over him, so that he might not deceive the nations any longer, *until the thousand years were ended. After that* he must be released for a little while" (Revelation 20:1-3). Chronologically, Satan will be bound *before* the millennial kingdom and then released *after* the millennial kingdom. The chronological clues are clear.

3. We also find very helpful chronological clues in Christ's prophetic Olivet Discourse (Matthew 24–25). For example, Jesus prophesied about the judgment of the nations in Matthew 25:31-46. There are chronological clues found in verses 31 and 32 that tell us when this judgment will occur. Notice the words I've italicized in the following passage: "*When* the Son of Man comes in his glory, and all the angels with him, *then* he will sit on his glorious throne. Before him will be gathered all the nations, and he will separate people one from another as a shepherd separates the sheep from the goats." Clearly, the judgment of the nations takes place right after the second coming of Christ. *When* Christ comes again, *then* He will judge the nations.

Once this judgment is complete, Christ will invite believers from among the nations into His 1,000-year millennial kingdom. How do we know this? The biblical text tells us that right after the judgment, "*Then* the King will say to those on his right, 'Come, you who are blessed by my Father, inherit the kingdom...'" (Matthew 25:34). The word *then* in this verse is another chronological clue.

4. Sometimes, chronological clues come in the form of theological inferences. Don't let that fancy phrase throw you. An "inference" is simply a conclusion reached on the basis of evidence and reasoning. So, a "theological inference" is a theological conclusion based on theological evidence and reasoning.

Allow me to illustrate this as it relates to the chronology of rebuilding the Jewish temple. We know from the book of Daniel that the antichrist will disallow Jewish sacrifices during the second half of the tribulation period—that is, the last three-and-a-half years of the seven-year tribulation period. This is explicitly stated in Daniel 9:27. Since the sacrifices will be *disallowed* during the second half, we can theologically infer that they will be *allowed* during the first half. That there will be sacrifices in the first half tells us there will be a temple at that time. After all, these sacrifices can *only* take place within a temple.

Another chronological clue that the temple will exist during the first half of the tribulation period is that Jesus said the tribulation temple would be desecrated: "When you see the abomination of desolation spoken of by the prophet Daniel, standing in the holy place...then let those who are in Judea flee to the mountains" (Matthew 24:15-16). This "abomination of desolation" will involve the desecration of the Jewish temple by the antichrist, who will set up an image of himself within the temple at the midpoint of the tribulation (2 Thessalonians 2:4). This means the temple must be rebuilt before the midpoint of the tribulation period.

Based on such chronological clues, we can "theologically infer" that the Jewish temple must be rebuilt during or before the first half of the tribulation period. That is one reason it is so exciting to see preparations being made *in our day* for rebuilding the temple. Money is being raised, architectural plans are being designed, and items used in temple worship are now being prefabricated.

5. The verse we just examined about the chronology of the rebuilding of the temple also reveals the chronology of the Jews' escape from Judea. Notice the words I've italicized in this passage: "*When* you see the abomination of desolation spoken of by the prophet Daniel, standing in the holy place...*then* let those who are in Judea flee to the mountains" (Matthew 24:15-16). *When* the temple is desecrated, *then* flee from Judea.

6. Many Christians are interested in how chronological clues relate to the timing of the rapture of the church—whether it is *before*, *during*, or *after* the tribulation period. I will cover all this in greater detail later in the book. But here is a brief summary to whet your appetite: (1) No Old Testament passage on the tribulation period mentions the church. (2) No New Testament passage on the tribulation period mentions the church. (3) The church is to be delivered from the wrath to come (1 Thessalonians 1:10). (4) The church is to be delivered from the actual *time period of trial* that is coming upon the entire world (Revelation 3:10). (5) God has a long track record of delivering His people before His judgments fall. (6) Scripture indicates that the rapture is imminent—meaning it could occur at any time (James 5:9). Based on these chronological clues, it is legitimate to theologically infer that the rapture will precede the tribulation period.

To sum up, we do not find an explicit timeline of prophetic events in the pages of Scripture. But we have chronological clues scattered throughout all the prophetic passages in the Bible. The accumulative total of all these chronological clues enables us to construct a reliable chronology of the end times. (You may wish to consult my book *The End Times in Chronological Order*, published by Harvest House Publishers.)

* * *

Many critics claim that Bible prophecy is sensationalistic and is therefore unworthy of serious attention. I believe this claim is inaccurate. Bible prophecy itself is not sensationalistic. Rather, some *interpreters* of Bible prophecy have engaged in sensationalism.

Sometimes sensationalism takes the form of airplanes dropping out of the sky at the rapture. Perhaps a more prevalent form of sensationalism involves the attempt of some to set dates for future prophetic events. Edgar C. Whisenant wrote a book entitled *88 Reasons Why the Rapture Will Be in 1988*. This 58-page book sold 4.5 million copies and stirred no small controversy in the church. The rapture, Whisenant claimed, would occur between September 11 and 13, 1988.

When Whisenant's predicted date for the rapture failed, he changed the September 11–13 date to October 3. When that date failed, he claimed it would be a few weeks later. When that didn't pan out, he claimed his calculations were off by a year and that Christ would return during Rosh Hashanah (September 30) in 1989, or perhaps at the end of the Feast of Tabernacles between October 14 and 20, 1989. *Wrong again!*

Whisenant is not alone. In his controversial book *1994?*, Harold Camping of Family Radio predicted that Jesus would return in September 1994. Camping claimed the likelihood of him being wrong on his calculations was very remote. He said he would be shocked if the world reached the year 2000. As I write, it is 2023.

Such date-setting triggered the "sensationalism alarm" in the minds of many critics. I must tell you that the sensationalism alarm also triggered—*at a deafening volume*—in my mind. That is why I wrote an article entitled "Millennial Madness" for the *Christian Research Journal* when Whisenant and Camping and others like them were claiming dates for the rapture. I wanted to warn Christians not to fall for the warped reasoning of these teachers.

Unfortunately, many critics wrongly assumed that Whisenant and Camping were representative of the general population of Christians. One can therefore understand why they leveled charges of sensationalism on such a broad scale.

The truth, however, is that despite the influence of Whisenant and Camping, *they were not representative of the general population of Christians*. Many Christians recognized that Whisenant and Camping departed from the clear teachings of Scripture: "It is not for you to know times or seasons that the Father has fixed by his own authority" (Acts 1:7). "Concerning that day and hour no one knows, not even the angels of heaven, nor the Son, but the Father only" (Matthew 24:36). Because many Christians followed the example of the Berean Christians in testing all claims against Scripture (Acts 17:11), they rejected the teachings of Whisenant and Camping and others like them. During my eight years on the *Bible Answer Man* radio broadcast, I was delighted to see how many Christians called in and cited such verses against date-setting.

Now, please allow me to switch gears for a moment: I find myself compelled to distinguish between *sensationalism* and *sensational*. Here is what I mean: When ancient prophecies uttered thousands of years ago come to pass in our day, *that is sensational*! An example is the rebirth of Israel. In the vision of dry bones in Ezekiel 37, the Lord is portrayed as miraculously bringing the bones back together into a skeleton, and the skeleton becomes wrapped in muscles, tendons, and flesh. God then breathes life into the body. There is no doubt that this chapter in Ezekiel is metaphorically speaking about Israel's rebirth, for we read: "Son of man, these bones are the whole house of Israel" (verse 11). Hence, this chapter portrays Israel as becoming a living, breathing nation, brought back from the dead, as it were. *That is sensational!*

Bible prophecy then predicts that following Israel's rebirth as a nation, many Jews would stream back to the Holy Land from all the nations of the world. God promised: "I will take you from the nations and gather you from all the countries and bring you into your own land" (Ezekiel 36:24). Ever since 1948, when Israel became a nation again, countless Jews have indeed streamed back to the Holy Land, just as predicted. *That is sensational!*

Scripture prophesies that sometime after this, there would be a significant invasion into Israel by Russia, Iran, Sudan, Turkey, Libya, and other Muslim nations (Ezekiel 38:1-6). While this invasion has not yet taken place, the stage is currently being set for it. Expansionist Russia already has military alliances with these nations, and the Muslims have plenty of motivation to attack Israel. Many believe—with good reason—that it is *sensational* that the ancient prophets were so "spot on" in their predictions of the end times.

So, here is my point: While we should never engage in *sensationalism* in Bible prophecy, there is certainly nothing wrong in recognizing how *sensational* God's fulfilled prophecies are. Such prophecies excite us about the coming of the Lord, whenever that event may occur.

There is one final balancing truth worthy of mention: Contrary to sensationalism, Scripture encourages us to be *serious-minded* about the end times. First Peter 4:7 explicitly instructs us: "The end of all things is at hand; therefore be self-controlled and sober-minded." The Holman Christian Standard Bible translates the latter part of the verse, "be serious and disciplined." The New King James Version puts it "be serious and watchful." The Amplified Bible renders it "keep sound-minded and self-controlled." Such words leave no room for sensationalism.

• • •

Some critics claim that Bible prophecy can distract Christians from more important matters, such as fulfilling the Great Commission. But wait a minute. More than one-fourth of the Bible is prophetic. Are we to conclude that this extensive portion of the Bible is a distraction from fulfilling the Great Commission? *What a bizarre claim!*

I believe Bible prophecy actually *contributes* to fulfilling the Great Commission. Prophecy can play a powerful role in evangelism. I am living proof of this. My exposure to Bible prophecy in the 1970s directly led to my conversion to Christ.

Prophecy was certainly used in the evangelistic sermon preached by Peter on the Day of Pentecost. People visiting Jerusalem had just witnessed people speaking in tongues—that is, speaking the gospel message in many languages that were recognized by various ethnic groups visiting Jerusalem from out of town. Peter promptly launched into his sermon by saying, "These people are not drunk, as you suppose, since it is only the third hour of the day. But this is what was uttered through the prophet Joel" (Acts 2:15). Peter then got specific about how the supernatural phenomena that occurred on the Day of Pentecost was a partial fulfillment of what Joel had prophesied so long ago. Following this, Peter launched into his evangelistic appeal, and 3,000 people became believers that day (Acts 2:41). *Peter effectively combined prophecy and evangelism.*

I once spent part of an afternoon with Hal Lindsey, author of the mega-seller *The Late Great Planet Earth*. I met with him just prior to his appearance on the *Bible Answer Man* radio broadcast. Hal has thousands of letters in his file cabinets from people who became Christians after reading his prophecy book. Given this, who can deny that prophecy can play a vital role in fulfilling the Great Commission?

Another example is how messianic prophecies have often been used in evangelizing Jewish people. From a prophetic standpoint, the Messiah had to become a human being (Genesis 3:15). He had to be Jewish—a descendant of Abraham, Isaac, and Jacob (Genesis 12:1-3). He had to come from the tribe of Judah (Genesis 49:10) and from David's family (2 Samuel 7:16). He had to be born in Bethlehem (Micah 5:2) of a virgin (Isaiah 7:14). He was to be despised and rejected by His fellow Jews, be put to death following a judicial proceeding, and be guiltless (Isaiah 53). These and countless other messianic prophecies are often used in an effective way in evangelism among Jewish people.

Contrary to being a distraction, Bible prophecy is a great help in fulfilling the Great Commission.

• • •

Critics sometimes allege that because Daniel 12:9 says prophecy is "sealed" until the end of time, no one can understand it until then. We should therefore not expend much time or effort studying prophecies like those in Daniel.

Let's consider the details of Daniel 12:9. This verse says that the prophetic words communicated to Daniel were to be "shut up and sealed until the time of the end." This verse means that the prophetic words recorded in Daniel were to be kept safe and preserved for future generations—especially for those who may be alive during the future tribulation days. At that time, the words would become particularly meaningful and understood. The Lord thus indicated to Daniel that much of what he had prophetically received would remain obscure until the end times. One Bible commentator summarizes the instructions to Daniel this way: "Daniel, go your way. Seal up this prophecy...The wise will understand at the right time. But Daniel, shut the book. It's not for your day."[1]

Of course, the sealing of Daniel's book does not mean we are to ignore this portion of the prophetic word in the Bible. While some of what Daniel wrote is reserved for full understanding in the end times, much of what Daniel wrote parallels the book of Revelation. The study of Daniel alongside Revelation can yield many insights into the end times. (See my books *40 Days Through Daniel* and *40 Days Through Revelation*, both published by Harvest House Publishers.)

Further, the sealing of Daniel's book certainly does not stand in the way of us studying other end-times prophecies in the Bible—for example, those found in Isaiah, Ezekiel, Zechariah, Matthew 24–25 (Christ's Olivet Discourse), John, 1 Corinthians, 2 Corinthians, 1 Thessalonians, 2 Thessalonians, and other books of the Bible. Daniel is one of many books in the Bible that contain prophecies of the end times. To dismiss *all* end-times prophecies because prophecies in a *single* prophetic book are "sealed" is as unwarranted as it is unwise.

Here is something important to think about: Many believe we are now living in the end times. This is indicated by the convergence of multiple prophecies being fulfilled in our day, or at least the stage is being set for their fulfillment. An example of a significant end-times prophecy being fulfilled is the rebirth of Israel as a nation (Ezekiel 37). If we are living in the end times, as I believe we are, then we ought to pay particular attention to the prophecies in Daniel. We are drawing closer to when these verses will come into full clarity.

• • •

Some have claimed that because Jesus said, "No one knows the day or the hour," we should not spend much effort or time studying Bible prophecy. This claim ultimately amounts to saying, "Because no one knows the day or the hour, we should not spend much effort or time studying one-fourth of the Bible." After all, one-fourth of the Bible is prophetic. I think this claim involves Satan-inspired logic, for Satan loves to keep people from the Word of God (Mark 4:15; Luke 8:12).

One who chooses not to study prophecy robs himself of special blessing. There are seven specific pronouncements of blessing in the book of Revelation. The first is found in 1:3: "Blessed is the one who reads aloud the words of this prophecy, and blessed are those who hear, and who keep what is written in it, for the time is near" (see also 14:13; 16:15; 19:9; 20:6; 22:7, 14). The word *blessed* means "spiritually happy." Since spiritual happiness comes from studying the prophecies in the book of Revelation, why would one choose not to study those prophecies?

The apostle Paul set the right example for us. He "did not shrink from declaring...*the whole counsel of God*" (Acts 20:27, emphasis added). Surely the "whole counsel of God" includes Bible prophecy.

If we as Christians want to understand the whole counsel of God, then Bible prophecy *must* be among the doctrines we study.

It is true that we cannot know the day or the hour of specific prophetic events. For example, we cannot say that the rapture of the church will take place on November 11, 2027, at 4:47 p.m. However, we can know that the rapture is an imminent event that could occur at any moment—even today (James 5:7-9). There is not a single prophecy that must be fulfilled before the occurrence of the rapture. That is why we call the rapture a "signless" event. There are no signs of the times that precede it.

In keeping with this, the apostle Paul affirmed that "time is running out" and "our salvation is nearer now than when we first believed" (Romans 13:11 NLT). Pretribs believe the word *salvation* in this context refers to the rapture, for Paul describes it as a specific future event. At the end of each day, the Christian is that much closer to the rapture. Paul thus exhorted that we "eagerly wait" for the Lord Jesus Christ (1 Corinthians 1:7 NKJV; Philippians 3:20 NKJV). We are now "waiting for our blessed hope, the appearing of the glory of our great God and Savior Jesus Christ" (Titus 2:13). Indeed, "the Lord is coming soon" (Philippians 4:5). We "are looking forward to the coming of God's Son from heaven" (1 Thessalonians 1:10 NLT). In other words, *we live in constant expectancy of Jesus coming to rapture us.* We don't know the day or the hour, but the Lord could come for us at any moment.

Scripture shows that while we cannot know the day or the hour of prophetic events, we can nevertheless know we are living *in the season* of the Lord's return. Speaking of the end times, Jesus instructed His followers: "Look at the fig tree, and all the trees. As soon as they come out in leaf, you see for yourselves and know that the summer is already near. So also, when you see these things taking place, you know that the kingdom of God is near" (Luke 21:29-31). This passage does not tell us we can know the day or the hour, but we can certainly know that the Lord's coming is drawing near when we witness certain "signs of the times."

Since this is true, it is unjustified to say we shouldn't study prophecy because we cannot know the day or the hour of the Lord's return. Just the opposite is true. Because we do not know the day or hour, *we need to be prepared for the Lord's coming at all times.* And the only way to be ready for His coming at all times is to study all that the Bible teaches about prophecy, and act accordingly.

Finally, let us not forget that prophecy has a life-changing effect. Those who await the Lord's return pursue purity and righteousness in their lives (Titus 2:13-14; Romans 13:11-14; 1 Peter 4:7-10; 2 Peter 3:10-14; 1 John 3:2-3). To cease studying Bible prophecy robs one of these life-changing benefits.

• • •

It is sobering that some Christian pastors are claiming we shouldn't waste time studying the rapture because there are so many interpretations of it—pretribulationism, posttribulationism, midtribulationism, the pre-wrath view, and the partial rapture theory.

In response, does this mean we should not study the book of Revelation since people hold to different views—the futurist view, the historicist view, the idealist view, and the preterist view? Does this mean we shouldn't study the millennium since people hold different views—premillennialism, amillennialism, and postmillennialism? Does this mean we should not study the biblical covenants since people hold different views—such as dispensationalism versus covenant theology?

For that matter, should we avoid studying all the other issues in Scripture where Christians have different viewpoints, such as the spiritual gifts, the nature of biblical inerrancy, the nature of sanctification, original sin and the fall, the extent of the atonement, God and the problem of evil, the role of women in the church, forms of church government, the use of musical instruments in church, the days of Genesis 1, the significance of the Lord's Supper, eternal punishment, water baptism, eternal security, the relationship of Israel and the church, Christianity and science, and the relationship of faith and reason?

As noted previously, the apostle Paul felt compelled to teach "the whole counsel of God" (Acts 20:27). He didn't cherry-pick what he thought people needed (or wanted) to hear. Rather, he taught the whole truth and nothing but the whole truth—including the truth about the rapture (1 Corinthians 15:50-51; 1 Thessalonians 4:13-18). The fact that there are five views of the rapture is not a reason to avoid studying the doctrine. On the contrary, it should motivate us to study the doctrine *all the more* so we can discern which of the five views is correct.

• • •

Liberal critics often claim that messianic prophecies of Christ's first coming were inserted into the Bible after the fact, and are therefore untrustworthy. This claim is flatly false. Scholars are practically unanimous that the Old Testament prophetic books were completed at least 400 years before Christ was even born, with many books dating as far back as the eighth and ninth centuries BC. The exception is the book of Daniel, which some scholars date to 167 BC. However, no matter whether a prophetic book dates 167 years before Christ's birth or 800 years, it is equally hard to predict a future event. For a prophecy to be fulfilled perfectly requires that it come from God alone, who knows the end from the beginning (Isaiah 46:10).

As an example, let us consider the book of Isaiah, written around 680 BC. This book is ideal for our purposes because it contains so many messianic prophecies.

In the early 1900s, the earliest available manuscript copy of Isaiah we had in our possession was dated at AD 980. Following the discovery of the Dead Sea Scrolls in 1947, scholars could examine a manuscript copy of Isaiah dated at 150 BC. This means that any specific prophecies of the coming divine Messiah that are recorded in Isaiah—including that Jesus would be born of a virgin (7:14), be called Immanuel (7:14), be anointed by the Holy Spirit (11:2), have a ministry in Galilee (9:1-2), have a ministry of miracles (35:5-6), be silent before His accusers (53:7), be crucified with thieves (53:12), accomplish a sacrificial atonement for humankind (53:5), and then be buried in a rich man's tomb (53:9)—cannot possibly have been recorded after the fact, as some have tried to claim. These prophecies—recorded in a manuscript dated at 150 BC—were fulfilled with pinpoint precision in the life of Jesus the Messiah. This attests to the existence of a supernatural God who alone has the ability to make accurate predictions hundreds of years in advance.

This supernatural God makes the following assertions in the book of Isaiah (pay special attention to the words I've put in italics):

- "Who is like me? Let him proclaim it. Let him declare and set it before me, since I appointed an ancient people. *Let them declare what is to come, and what will happen*" (Isaiah 44:7).

- "*Have I not told you from of old and declared it?* And you are my witnesses! Is there a God besides me? There is no Rock; I know not any" (Isaiah 44:8).

- "*Who declared it of old? Was it not I, the LORD?* And there is no other god besides me" (Isaiah 45:21).

- "*The former things I declared of old; they went out from my mouth, and I announced them; then suddenly I did them, and they came to pass...I declared them to you from of old, before they came to pass I announced them to you*, lest you should say, 'My idol did them, my carved image and my metal image commanded them'" (Isaiah 48:3, 5).

Of course, anyone can make predictions—that is easy. Having them fulfilled is another story altogether. The more statements you make about the future, and the greater the detail, the better the chances are that you will be proven wrong. *But God was never wrong.* All the Old Testament messianic prophecies about Christ's first coming—most of them dating at least 400 years before the time of Christ—were explicitly fulfilled in the person of Jesus Christ. None of the prophecies were adjusted after the fact.

• • •

Liberal critics sometimes claim that Jesus' disciples manipulated His life so that He appeared to fulfill messianic prophecies when He actually did not. This claim does not fit the biblical facts. The writers of Scripture were God-fearing Jews who gave every evidence of possessing the highest moral character, each having been raised since early childhood to obey the Ten Commandments—including the commandment against bearing false witness (Exodus 20:16). It breaches all credulity to say that these men were deceitful and sought to fool people into believing Jesus was the Messiah when He really was not. It also breaches credulity to suggest that these men chose to suffer and even give up their lives as martyrs in defense of what they knew to be a lie.

Further, there are many prophecies fulfilled in the person of Jesus that the biblical writers could not have manipulated, such as His being born in Bethlehem (Micah 5:2), His direct descent from David (2 Samuel 7:12-16) and Abraham (Genesis 12:2), His being born of a virgin (Isaiah 7:14), the identity of His forerunner, John the Baptist (Malachi 3:1), the Sanhedrin's gift of 30 pieces of silver to Judas, the betrayer (Zechariah 11:12), the soldiers gambling for His clothing (Psalm 22:18), His legs remaining unbroken (Psalm 22:17), and other prophecies.

Still further, related to prophecies of Jesus' resurrection from the dead (Psalm 16:10; 22:22), it is unlikely that the writers of Scripture could have stolen the body to give the appearance of a resurrection. After all, the tomb was blocked by an enormous stone weighing several tons. It also bore the seal of the Roman government—with an automatic death penalty for anyone who breached it. The tomb was also guarded by Roman soldiers trained in defense and killing. To say Jesus' Jewish followers overcame these guards, moved the enormous stone, and stole the body is not a credible scenario. Not only is it not credible, but the biblical evidence indicates that Jesus' followers scattered like a bunch of spineless cowards after Jesus' arrest: "They all deserted him and ran away" (Mark 14:50 csb). They were in no frame of mind to do battle with trained Roman soldiers in order to take the body of Jesus.

* * *

It is possible that some of the claims I address in this chapter may have initially seemed convincing to you. In each case, however, I have shown how these claims are easily answered. This illustrates something Solomon once said: "The one who states his case first seems right, until the other comes and examines him" (Proverbs 18:17). In the next chapter, we will consider some of today's most common claims against the pretribulational rapture.

2

THE PRETRIBULATIONAL RAPTURE IN THE CROSSHAIRS

Years ago, when I was a student at Dallas Theological Seminary, I had a fascinating discussion about the pretribulational rapture with Dr. John F. Walvoord, one of the truly great defenders of the doctrine. Walvoord wrote the book *The Rapture Question*, which is an academic treatment of the subject. It is considered the definitive book on the pretrib rapture and is often used as a textbook at Bible colleges and seminaries.

During our discussion, I asked Dr. Walvoord, "What would you do if you found yourself in the tribulation period?" He paused for a moment, and with a slight smile beginning to form at the edges of his mouth said, "I think I might write a new book titled *Rethinking the Rapture*."

That's one thing I loved about Walvoord. He always had such a good sense of humor. He is now with the Lord in heaven. I will see him again at the rapture (1 Thessalonians 4:13-18).

Even though Walvoord is no longer with us on earth, he continues to be a target of criticism by posttribulationists, midtribulation-ists, preterists, proponents of the pre-wrath view, and proponents of the partial rapture view. I think I can speak for most other pretrib authors—including the likes of John Ankerberg, Mark Hitchcock, David Jeremiah, Thomas Ice, and Jan Markell—in saying that we are all targets of criticism. Writing prophecy books—especially books on the pretrib rapture—is not for the faint of heart.

In what follows, I will address some of the more common arguments and claims against the pretribulational rapture. Keep in mind that this chapter is introductory, and I will address further arguments against the rapture later in the book. In chapter 8, for example, I will address the preterist case against pretribulationism. In chapter 9, I will address church history and whether it is a friend or foe of pretribulationism. In chapters 10 and 11, I will consider alternative views of the rapture—and what they say about pretribulationism.

• • •

We begin with the common claim that there is no reference in the Bible to a "secret rapture" or a "secret coming" of Christ at the rapture. Therefore, critics say the rapture is an unbiblical doctrine.

It is true that there is not a single reference in the Bible to a "secret rapture" or a "secret coming" of Christ at the rapture. However, there are two theological factors that sometimes give rise to talk about a "secret rapture": (1) First Corinthians 15:52 tells us that the rapture will take place "in the twinkling of an eye." (2) Believers will be caught up "in the clouds to meet the Lord in the air" (1 Thessalonians 4:17). It will be *instant*. We will be taken *far up in the air*.

Despite these theological facts, the rapture will be anything but a secret. With millions vanishing off the planet in the blink of an eye, people all over the world will be grasping for answers. This event will probably make global headlines. Videos of people vanishing will no doubt go viral on the internet.

The late Ed Hindson, in his inspiring book *Future Glory*, writes:

> Those who have rejected the salvation of Jesus Christ
> and remain on earth will witness a miraculous event of
> astonishing proportions—the sudden mass disappearance
> of millions upon millions of Christians from the face of
> the earth. While critics of the rapture teaching often object
> to it as a "secret rapture," there won't be anything secret
> about it! The unbelieving world will be in a state of shock.[1]

It is likely that many who are "left behind" at the rapture will
remember what their Christian friends and family members said
about the rapture. Hence, it is entirely possible that many people will
become believers in Jesus after witnessing this event. It may also be
that the two mighty prophets of Revelation 11, and the 144,000 Jewish witnesses of Revelation 7 and 14, may refer to the mass vanishing
that took place at the rapture as they share the gospel of the kingdom
with people. We know there will be many conversions because Revelation 7 refers to a great multitude of believers who come "out of the
great tribulation" (verse 14). This *not-so-secret* rapture may be used by
these spokesmen for God in their evangelistic appeals.

• • •

Pretribulationists often teach that no Scripture passage mentions
the church as being on earth during the tribulation period. They
believe this supports their view that the rapture will precede the tribulation period.

Posttribulationists turn the tables and rebut that the church is
not mentioned as being *in heaven* during this time. They say that
not one verse in Revelation 4–19 says the church is in heaven. They
argue that if the church was in heaven during the tribulation period,
surely there would be at least one verse that explicitly says so.

At first glance, this seems to be a good argument against pretribulationism. However, I urge you to remember what Solomon said: "The one who states his case first seems right, until the other comes and examines him" (Proverbs 18:17).

It is true that there is no explicit mention of "the church" in heaven in Revelation 4–19. No one denies that. What posttribulationists fail to appreciate, however, is that there is also no explicit mention of "the church" in heaven *in the eternal state*, even though we know all believers are in heaven in the eternal state (Revelation 21–22). If we were to be consistent in using posttrib reasoning, we'd have to say that if the church were in heaven in the eternal state, then surely there would be at least one verse in the book of Revelation that explicitly says the church is there. But no such verse exists.

Of course, such reasoning is fallacious. Pretribs believe that just as the church is in heaven in the eternal state (even though the church is not explicitly mentioned as being in heaven), so the church is also in heaven during the tribulation period, which follows the rapture (even though the church is not explicitly mentioned as being in heaven during this time).

There are certainly some scriptural indications that the church is indeed in heaven during the tribulation period, even though the word *church* is not mentioned. For example, the "saints" are in heaven during the tribulation period. After evil Babylon is destroyed toward the end of the tribulation, we find the following exhortation to rejoice for those who are in heaven: "Rejoice over her, O heaven, and you saints and apostles and prophets, for God has given judgment for you against her" (Revelation 18:20). The "saints" in heaven refers specifically to redeemed human beings, which certainly includes the church.

That the "saints" are in heaven during the tribulation period recalls the promise of Christ Himself in John 14:2-3: "In my Father's house are many rooms. If it were not so, would I have told you that I go to prepare a place for you? And if I go and prepare a place for you, I will come again and will take you to myself, that where I am you may be also." This passage shows that immediately following the rapture, Christ will take all believers—all the "saints"—directly to heaven so they can be with Him always.

Also, let us not forget that the book of Revelation contains many symbols. I mention this because many Bible expositors believe the reference to the twenty-four elders in Revelation 4–5 symbolizes the church. How do we know this? These elders are portrayed as having crowns on their heads at the very start of the tribulation period (Revelation 4:4). It seems logical to surmise that if the elders represent the church, and if they already have crowns early in the tribulation period, then they must have faced the judgment seat of Christ right after the rapture. Scripture elsewhere portrays the rewards believers will receive at the judgment seat of Christ as crowns—the crown of life (James 1:12; Revelation 2:10), the crown of glory (1 Peter 5:4), the crown imperishable (1 Corinthians 9:25), and the crown of righteousness (2 Timothy 4:8).

Critics of pretribulationism respond that there is a problem with this view. Theologian Charles Ryrie, in his book *Come Quickly, Lord Jesus*, summarizes the problem and explains why it is not really a problem after all:

> Some think this argument is no good because the critical text of [Revelation] 5:9-10 has the elders singing about redemption *in the third person*, as if redemption were not their own experience (thus they could not represent the church, which has been redeemed). But this is a weak argument; after all, Moses sang of redemption in the third person, right after he experienced it (Exodus 15:13, 16, 17).[2]

To be more specific, Moses, addressing God, spoke of the redeemed in the third person: "You have led in your steadfast love the people whom you have redeemed; you have guided them by your strength to your holy abode" (Exodus 15:13). This wording may make it seem as if redemption was not Moses' experience, when in fact he was among the redeemed. Likewise, in Revelation 5:9-10, the 24 elders address the Redeemer Jesus Christ and speak of the redeemed in the third person: "You were slain, and by your blood you ransomed people for God from every tribe and language and people and nation, and you have made them a kingdom and priests to our God, and they shall reign on the earth." Just as Moses was among the redeemed, and yet spoke in the third person, so the 24 elders were apparently among the redeemed, even though they too spoke in the third person.

In keeping with all of this, Scripture reveals that at the second coming of Christ, which follows the tribulation period, the bride of Christ (the church) will return with Him (Revelation 19:14). The church, as Christ's bride, will be adorned in "fine linen, bright and pure" (19:8). Such apparel shows that these believers have already passed through the judgment seat of Christ (see 3:5).

We conclude that while the church is not explicitly mentioned as being in heaven in Revelation 4–19, the church's presence there is explicitly recognized as "the saints" and the "bride of Christ," and is symbolized by the 24 elders.

* * *

Some posttrib critics of pretribulationism believe the reason Scripture reveals so much about the tribulation period is that Christians will go through it. There are significant problems with this viewpoint:

1. One might ask, "Does the fact that Scripture tells us a lot about hell mean that Christians will be there?" Of course not! Likewise, the fact that Scripture tells us a lot about the tribulation period does not mean Christians will be there.

2. God sometimes speaks of His impending judgment to people even though those people will not themselves go through the period of judgment. This certainly applies to God's revelation to Christians about eternal suffering in hell (for example, Matthew 13:50; 25:46; 2 Thessalonians 1:9; 2 Peter 2:4; Jude 1:7; Revelation 21:8). This is also illustrated in Genesis 18, where God revealed to Abraham that He was about to destroy the wicked cities of Sodom and Gomorrah. This judgment did not directly affect Abraham in any way, though it moved him to pray as a result of God's revelation to him.

3. The reality of a coming tribulation period can be a powerful motivation to engage in evangelism and missionary work. Perhaps that's one reason God tells us so much about what the future holds for unbelievers. The more people that can be delivered from this time of God's wrath, the better. The horror of the tribulation period casts the Great Commission into a whole new light: "Go therefore and make disciples of all nations, baptizing them in the name of the Father and of the Son and of the Holy Spirit, teaching them to observe all that I have commanded you. And behold, I am with you always, to the end of the age" (Matthew 28:19-20). Time is of the essence. We must reach people for Christ and do it quickly!

4. There will be a great multitude of people who become believers during the tribulation period (Revelation 7:9-17). Even though they will face severe persecution, and in some cases martyrdom, they will gain great strength and comfort in reading and understanding prophetic Scripture, particularly the prophecies relating to the tribulation period, the second coming, the millennial kingdom, and the eternal state.

Therefore, the fact that such revelation about the tribulation period is in the Bible does not demand or imply that the church will go through the tribulation period.

5. Bible prophecy shows the greatness of God. In Isaiah 41:21-24, God challenges the false gods regarding their inability to prophesy the future like He can. God demonstrated that these "gods" are, in fact, not gods at all but are dead idols. Even if the church does not go through the tribulation period (as I believe Scripture teaches), what we learn about the tribulation period in prophecy is a testament to God's uniqueness and greatness. People who become Christians during the tribulation period will definitely appreciate learning about God's true greatness, even as they witness the antichrist's *pretense* of greatness.

6. The book of Revelation teaches us a great deal about the sinfulness of humanity, the holiness and wrath of God, the agenda of Satan, and the glorious fact that God's gospel light will continue to shine even in the darkest period of human history—the tribulation period. The fact that such revelation about the tribulation period is in the Bible does not demand or imply that the church will be there, but rather, may have an educational purpose.

7. Finally, as is true with all Bible prophecy, the prophecies about the tribulation period inspire believers toward consecrated holy living (Revelation 2–3; see also Titus 2:13-14; Romans 13:11-14; Titus 2:13-14; 1 Peter 4:7-10; 2 Peter 3:10-14; 1 John 3:2-3). This revelation about the tribulation period should not be taken to mean the church will be there, but rather, motivates righteousness in the lives of all who are a part of the church.

• • •

Some posttribulationists reason that because believers are to be alert for the "Day of the Lord," they apparently will experience this day of God's wrath. We find this instruction in 1 Thessalonians 5:1-11. Verse 6, in particular, urges us: "So then let us not sleep, as others do, but let us keep awake and be sober." If believers are exhorted to "keep awake and be sober," then they must go through the tribulation period. This means pretribulationism cannot be correct.

I do not believe this accurately reflects the teaching of Scripture. There is no need to assume the church will go through the tribulation period simply because Christians are urged to stay awake and be sober as that day of judgment nears. It makes sense for God to urge us to be sober in view of the devastation that will one day be visited upon our earth, our cities, and our neighborhoods—even if we also know we'll be raptured before the day arrives. One's thinking might go something like this: *My city—the city where I have lived for decades, the city where I have raised my children—will be crushed by the three sets of devastating judgments that will fall upon this earth. I won't be here. But many people will be here—likely including some people I know. And my city will face the devastation of wars, plagues, destruction by fire, famine, massive death, water turned into blood, and much more. My city won't be spared. My neighborhood won't be spared. I am excited about the rapture, but the destruction that is coming in the "Day of the Lord" is heartbreaking and sobering.* This is what I believe is being communicated in 1 Thessalonians 5:1-11. Therefore, this passage does not pack the punch against pretribulationism that some posttribs surmise that it does.

• • •

Some critics are sure there can be no imminent pretribulational rapture because the resurrection will occur on "the last day." Jesus declared: "This is the will of my Father, that everyone who looks on the Son and believes in him should have eternal life, and I will raise him up on the last day" (John 6:40). If the resurrection will be "on the last day," then a pretribulational rapture—an *imminent* rapture—seems out of the question.

Let us note at the outset that if this verse is a problem for pretribulationism, it is also a problem for midtribulationism, posttribulationism, the pre-wrath view, and the partial-rapture view. After all, if the phrase "last day" absolutely demands that the resurrection takes place at the eschatological end of time, then this would place the rapture far beyond all these views.

But what if "the last day" does not refer to the virtual end of God's eschatological timeline? What if it means something else?

Interestingly, most references to "the last day" occur in John 6, where Jesus is speaking specifically about the resurrection:

> *John 6:39*—"This is the will of him who sent me, that I should lose nothing of all that he has given me, but raise it up on the last day."

> *John 6:40*—"This is the will of my Father, that everyone who looks on the Son and believes in him should have eternal life, and I will raise him up on the last day."

> *John 6:44*—"No one can come to me unless the Father who sent me draws him. And I will raise him up on the last day."

> *John 6:54*—"Whoever feeds on my flesh and drinks my blood has eternal life, and I will raise him up on the last day."

Because most verses that mention "the last day" are connected to the future resurrection—*and* because the resurrection takes place in connection with the rapture ("the dead in Christ will rise first"—1 Thessalonians 4:16)—it is possible to view "the last day" as being the actual day of the rapture. Proponents of this view reason that the church age began on the Day of Pentecost and ends on the day of the rapture. So, perhaps the day of the rapture itself is "the last day" of the church age dispensation, at which time dead believers are resurrected. If this view is correct, then the rapture can still be considered imminent. It could take place at any time.

Others believe that perhaps "the last day" refers to the final day a believer has a mortal body. (Again, keep in mind that most of the references to "the last day" take place in John 6 and relate to the resurrection.) At the rapture, dead believers will be resurrected and living believers will be instantly translated into their eternal glorified bodies. In this view, the last day is something to look forward to with great anticipation since the frailties of the mortal earthly body will become a thing of the past. If this view is correct, then the rapture may still be considered imminent. It could take place at any time.

While these views are possible, I've concluded that "the last day" is not a specific 24-hour day, but rather, is an extended day of prophetic fulfillment in the end times, during which various prophetic events take place, including the rapture, resurrection, and judgment. We've already seen that the term "the last day" is used in connection with the resurrection in the Gospel of John (see 6:39, 40, 44, 54). But it is also used in connection with judgment (12:48). If "the last day" is an extended day of prophetic fulfillment, then the verse does not disallow pretribulationism or any of the other rapture views. The correct view of the rapture must be determined on other grounds and not based on this verse.

A basic interpretive principle is that we should always interpret the difficult verses in light of what the easier and clearer verses teach. I believe the preponderance of clear verses strongly supports pretribulationism.

• • •

Some posttrib critics allege that pretribulationism gives people a false hope. If a person believes in pretribulationism, and that view ends up being incorrect, then that person will be spiritually unprepared for what he or she will encounter during the tribulation period. Pretribulationism therefore produces a false hope and is setting Christians up for a fall. Posttribs claim we ought to be preparing Christians for survival during the tribulation period.

I believe this criticism is invalid for the following reasons:

1. This argument falsely assumes that pretribulationism is incorrect. As we see in this book, however, there is strong theological support for pretribulationism (see chapter 12, "The Biblical Case for the Pretribulational Rapture").

2. Our basis of spiritual truth is the Bible alone, not a fear-driven speculative scenario of Christians allegedly being unprepared for the tribulation period.

3. In the unlikely event that pretribulationism proves to be incorrect, then pretribulational Christians will be sustained by the Lord (Psalm 55:22; 73:26; Isaiah 40:29, 31; 41:10; Nahum 1:7; Philippians 4:13; 1 Peter 5:7). Further, we are spiritually refueled daily by spending time meditating on Scripture, not by meditating on our theological model. Immersing ourselves in the Scriptures helps to produce in us an eternal perspective that gives us spiritual strength (see Colossians 3:1-2; compare with Revelation 21–22). As my old friend Walter Martin used to put it, "I read the last chapter in the book, *and we win!*"

4. Scripture points to a "great multitude" of people who will become Christians during the tribulation period. As Mark Hitchcock observes, "If these brand-new baby believers are

able to trust in the Lord even in the face of martyrdom, why would we doubt God's sufficiency to help the rest of us make it through?"[3]

5. It is telling that posttribulational leaders are not doing anything to prepare believers for survival in the tribulation period. They charge pretribs with setting Christians up for a fall during the tribulation period, while they themselves do nothing to prepare people for survival in the tribulation period! Is this fair?

6. Pretribulationists believe that our primary preparation involves being ready for the rapture, which could occur at any moment. Those who take this seriously will seek to live righteously.

7. There are virtually no instructions in the Bible regarding how church-age believers should prepare for entrance into the tribulation period. To clarify, the Bible *does* include teachings that are spiritually beneficial to "tribulation saints"— people who become Christians during the tribulation period. The parable of the ten bridesmaids in Matthew 25:1-13 is one such example. But church-age believers will have been raptured prior to the beginning of the tribulation period.

8. No matter what happens in the future, trust in the Lord. It is wise to always remember this proverb: "Trust in the LORD with all your heart, and do not lean on your own understanding. In all your ways acknowledge him, and he will make straight your paths" (Proverbs 3:5-6).

• • •

Some posttrib critics claim that pretribs make far too much of the "signs of the times"—especially as related to the alleged nearness of the rapture. In response, pretribulationists emphasize the signs of the times because prophetic Scripture emphasizes the signs of the times.

A key sign of the times—what we might call a "super sign"—is the rebirth of Israel as a nation in 1948. Ezekiel 37 clearly prophesied this rebirth. Ezekiel also prophesied that following Israel's rebirth, Jews from all over the world would stream back to Israel (Ezekiel 36:24). This has been happening ever since 1948. Ezekiel then prophesied a massive invasion into Israel by Russia, Iran, Turkey, Sudan, Libya, and other Muslim nations (Ezekiel 38:1-6). This invasion has not happened yet, but the stage is currently being set for it. Russia already has alliances with these various Muslim nations, and they have plenty of motive to attack Israel (see my book *Northern Storm Rising: Russia, Iran, and the Emerging End-Times Military Coalition Against Israel*, Harvest House Publishers). The point I am making is that the signs of the times are relevant to us because these signs are an indicator of the end times.

We don't want to make the same mistake made by the first-century Jews. Unlike them, we should seek to be accurate observers of the times. Consider these words from the Gospel of Matthew:

> The Pharisees and Sadducees came up, and testing Jesus, they asked Him to show them a sign from heaven. But He replied to them, "When it is evening, you say, 'It will be fair weather, for the sky is red.' And in the morning, 'There will be a storm today, for the sky is red and threatening.' Do you know how to discern the appearance of the sky, but cannot discern the signs of the times?" (Matthew 16:1-3 NASB1995).

What a rebuke! These guys—the Pharisees and the Sadducees, the religious elite of the time—were supposed to know the teachings of prophetic Scripture, and yet they were completely blind to properly discerning the times. They had been literally inundated by prophetic signs relating to Jesus being the divine Messiah, and they had missed them all. They were blinded to the reality that the Messiah was in their midst. The miracles Jesus wrought were just as clear a sign to His divine identity as dark clouds in the sky are a sign of impending rain. Jesus' miracles—sight for the blind, hearing for the deaf, and the like—had been prophesied of the Messiah in the Old Testament (Isaiah 35:5-6), and the Pharisees and Sadducees (experts in the Old Testament) should have seen Jesus as being the fulfillment of these messianic verses. But in their blindness, they could not "discern the signs of the times." So, again, we ought to resolve not to follow their example.

Many wonder what the relationship is between the signs of the times and the rapture. After all, the signs of the times deal specifically with the tribulation period. Here is the significance: If we witness the stage currently being set for a prophecy relating to the future tribulation period (such as the rebuilding of the Jewish temple, or the development of a one-world digital currency, or the movement toward globalism), then that fact would seem to be an indicator that the rapture is not far off, since the rapture precedes the tribulation period. *If the tribulation is near, then the rapture is even nearer.* Still, we should never set dates for prophetic events.

• • •

Some critics of pretribulationism note that the Bible calls the rapture a "mystery." They surmise that because the rapture is *mysterious*, we cannot have firm convictions about it.

This claim is based on a faulty understanding of what the Bible means by "mystery." A mystery, in the biblical sense, is a truth that cannot be discerned simply by human investigation but requires special revelation from God. The word refers to a truth that was unknown to people living in Old Testament times but is now revealed to humankind by God (Matthew 13:17; Colossians 1:26). While the idea of a resurrection was taught in Old Testament times (Job 19:25-26; Isaiah 26:19; Daniel 12:2), the idea that living believers on earth would be instantly translated into glorified bodies—thereby completely bypassing death—was a completely new truth not previously revealed. It is for this reason that the rapture is called a mystery.

To be clear, then, the rapture is not mysterious in the sense of being confusing or enigmatic. Rather, the rapture is a mystery in that it was a new revelation in New Testament times.

• • •

Some anti-rapture critics suggest we should not waste time on the rapture because it is such a divisive issue in the church.

In response:

1. Does this mean we should avoid virtually every doctrine where Christians are divided over the correct interpretation? If so, we'll have to ignore a considerable portion of the Bible. The divided opinions Christians have on various doctrines has given rise to many books: *Three Views on the Rapture, Four Views on Heaven, Five Views on Biblical Inerrancy, Three Views on the New Testament Use of the Old Testament, Five Views on Apologetics, Four Views on the Book of Revelation, Three Views on the Millennium and Beyond, Five Views on Law and Gospel, Five Views on Sanctification, Four Views on Divine Providence, Four Views on Eternal Security, Four Views on Christian Spirituality, Four Views on the Role of Works at the Final Judgment,* and many more. It is simply unreasonable to suggest that study of the rapture should be avoided because it is a potentially divisive issue. The fact that there are a number of views of the rapture should compel us all the more to study the Bible

so we can discover which view is correct. And we can do so without dividing from other Christians who see things differently. We can have *diversity* without *divisiveness.* We can follow the age-old maxim, "In essentials, unity; in non-essentials, liberty; and in all things, charity." The actual timing of the rapture—while very important—is considered a nonessential doctrine by Christian theologians. (It is considered a nonessential because one's salvation does not hinge on it.) So, we can *agree to disagree in an agreeable way* with our brothers and sisters who see things differently regarding the timing of the rapture.

2. We are wise to follow the example set by the apostle Paul, who taught "the whole counsel of God" (Acts 20:27). "The whole counsel of God" includes Bible prophecy.

3. Let us not forget that one-fourth of the Bible was prophetic when written—including many verses about the rapture. We should not ignore such a large portion of Scripture.

• • •

The most common claims against a pretribulational rapture are unfounded. We will see in this book that there is not only a forceful scriptural case for the pretrib rapture, but the objections against it are easily answered. In the next chapter, we will shift our attention to allegations against pretribulational Christians.

3

TARGETING PRETRIBULATIONAL CHRISTIANS

One of the largest newspapers in Southern California once interviewed me. It became apparent rather quickly that the interviewer I was talking to was not a Christian, but a rank secularist. At one point, after I made a comment on Christian doctrine, she asked, with a subtle undertone of condescension: "And you actually *believe* that?" Her line of questioning was definitely heading in the direction of casting Christians in a "neanderthal" light. So, I exited the interview politely and as quickly as possible. I had no intention of providing her with more comments to mock.

What is even more disturbing than a secularist mocking Christianity are Christians who speak with condescension and disdain about fellow Christians simply because they have different views on prophecy. It is one thing to take aim at *pretribulationism*. It is another thing entirely to target *pretribulationists*. Claims are engineered to make pretribs look silly, uninformed, or just plain dumb. It is unfortunate to see such tactics, but all this is part and parcel of prophecy under siege.

On the one hand, I dislike writing this chapter because the subject matter is distasteful. On the other hand, it is necessary to accurately portray the nature of prophecy under siege. So, in what follows, I will provide a representative sampling of the kinds of claims being made against pretribulationists. I will not, however, mention the names of critics. My goal is not to call attention to specific people but to deal with the uncharitable comments they are making.

• • •

Some critics of pretribulationism engage in *argumentum ad hominem*. This is a Latin phrase meaning "argument to the person." In modern vernacular, this is argumentation that attacks the character, motives, or personal attributes of the person making an argument rather than addressing the substance of the argument itself. An example of this type of argumentation is that Christians in my theological camp have been called "dreadfully superficial," "a cult," and they advocate "the most dangerous heresy."[1] These descriptive terms are as unfair as they are untrue. And they are highly offensive. Such comments are nothing short of a character assassination. But, my friend, it gets worse.

Critics charge that pretribs are guilty of "aggressive sophistry and fanatic exegesis" and engage in "paltry reasoning." Pretribs prefer "any rubbish to the true and obvious explanation" of a Scripture passage, and they "wrest the scriptures." They show "little acquaintance with great exegesis." Their teaching is "inconsistent and ludicrous" in its "absurdity." They are "misguided and misleading teachers." They display "weak-kneed, invertebrate, spineless sentiment" in their goal "of escaping tribulation."[2]

Such comments are unworthy of a response. Suffice it to say that those making these comments have attacked and slandered the character of many godly men and women who have prayerfully come to believe that pretribulationism is the correct biblical view. Whether the critics are posttribulationists, preterists, or advocates of one of the other positions, Dr. John F. Walvoord is right in saying that the *ad hominem* approach ultimately "does their cause more harm than good and raises the question as to why such an approach is used if their doctrine has a sound exegetical basis."[3]

It is especially unfortunate that these *ad hominem* statements are uttered by those who claim to be Christians. J.C. Ryle provides some appropriate words that were first uttered more than 100 years ago but are still incredibly relevant to our day:

> I must enter my protest against the sneering, taunting, contemptuous language which has been frequently used of late…To say the least, such language is unseemly, and only defeats its own end. A cause which is defended by such language is deservedly suspicious. Truth needs no such weapons. If we cannot agree with men, we need not speak of their views with discourtesy and contempt.[4]

Ryle thus urges: "Let us exercise charity in our judgments of one another," noting that to "exhibit bitterness and coldness" toward those who disagree with us on some matter "is to prove ourselves very ignorant of real holiness."[5]

I can only say, "Amen," to Ryle's words.

* * *

Despite how clearly, I think, 1 Thessalonians 4 speaks about the rapture, there are critics who claim that no legitimate and highly regarded biblical scholar has ever interpreted 1 Thessalonians 4 as a proof for the rapture. The implication is that only poor scholars support this view.

This is both a biblical argument and an *argumentum ad hominem* at the same time. While the argument focuses on 1 Thessalonians 4, it also impugns the character of pretribulational scholars (implying they are *poor* scholars).

In truth, there are many scholars of fine caliber who have held to pretribulationism, all of which cite 1 Thessalonians 4 in favor of their view. These include: A.J. Gordon (1836–1895), James M. Gray (1851–1935), R.A. Torrey (1856–1928), Arno C. Gaebelein (1861–1945), Lewis Sperry Chafer (1871–1952), Harry Ironside (1876–1951), John F. Strombeck (1881–1959), Alva J. McClain (1888–1968), Charles Lee Feinberg (1909–1995), John F. Walvoord (1910–2002), J. Dwight Pentecost (1915–2014), Charles C. Ryrie (1925–2016), and Norman L. Geisler (1932–2019). Bible colleges and seminaries where pretribulationism is taught include such fine institutions as Moody Bible Institute, Biola University, Philadelphia Biblical University (renamed Cairn University in 2012), Dallas Theological Seminary, Grace Theological Seminary, Liberty University, Bob Jones University, and The Master's University and Seminary.

Might I suggest that instead of attacking the character of other Christians, it is better to keep our focus on what Scripture teaches? It will not do to simply categorize scholars who believe in pretribulationism as "*poor* scholars." Pretribulationists could just as easily respond by declaring that those who deny a rapture in 1 Thessalonians 4 are poor scholars. But such back-and-forth accusations are not only silly, they get us nowhere. This is all the more reason to keep our focus on Scripture. By following this approach, we can all generate more light than heat in our theological discussions.

* * *

Some posttribulational critics charge that pretribs have come down with a severe case of escapism. Pretribs allegedly have a pathological desire to escape the tribulation period. They are "deathly afraid" to go through any part of the tribulation, and this motivates their escapism. We are told that pretribs just need to "get over it."

Walvoord makes an interesting point on this issue:

> Is it an unworthy motive to desire to escape the Great
> Tribulation? Actually, it is no more so than the desire to

escape hell. The point in either case is not our desire or wishes but the question as to what the Scriptures promise. Pretribulationists hope to escape the Great Tribulation because it is expressly a time of divine judgment on a world that has rejected Christ.[6]

While I do not want to go through the tribulation period, I can say with absolute certainty in my heart that I am a pretribulationist *not* because I am an escapist who is afraid to go through the tribulation but because I am convinced that this is what Scripture teaches (see chapter 12, "The Biblical Case for the Pretribulational Rapture"). If I believed Scripture taught posttribulationism, I would have no qualms about going through the tribulation period because of my assurance that, no matter what, I will be with the Lord within seven years—or sooner if I get martyred.

• • •

A charge that has circulated for a long time is that pretribulationists are so heavenly minded that they ignore the critical social problems that need fixing in our day. Pretribs are allegedly so *otherworld focused* that they have no sensitivity to *this-world problems.*

I don't think this claim is true. Speaking of Christians in general (and not specifically pretribulationists), C.S. Lewis commented: "If you read history you will find that the Christians who did most for the present world were just those who thought most of the next…It is since Christians have largely ceased to think of the other world that they have become so ineffective in this."[7] I think Lewis's words ring true of pretribulationists. I've attended pretribulational churches for decades, and in each case, the church was not only concerned about, *but took specific action regarding* various social issues in its immediate vicinity.

One thing critics forget is that pretribulationists believe that immediately following the rapture, Christians will face the judgment seat of Christ. Christians will be judged on how they lived during their short years on earth. Pretribulationists recognize that among the likely issues that will come up at this judgment is how they helped other people in need. For example, a common social problem is that people sometimes run out of money and cannot buy food for their families. In such cases, the church lends a helping hand by providing the funds. Churches also support local downtown missions that provide food and shelter for the homeless. Further, many churches pitch in to help the sick who cannot afford to pay all their medical bills. These and many other similar examples show that pretribs are indeed concerned about the social difficulties that face them.

The fact that we are "heavenly minded" motivates our social actions. J.I. Packer—who himself was not a pretribulationist—once said that the "lack of long, strong thinking about our promised hope of glory is a major cause of our plodding, lackluster lifestyle."[8] Packer pointed to the Puritans as a much-needed example for us, for they believed that "it is the heavenly Christian that is the lively Christian."[9] The Puritans understood that we "run so slowly, and strive so lazily because we so little mind the prize…So let Christians animate themselves daily to run the race set before them by practicing heavenly meditation."[10] It is the lively Christian—the spiritually animated Christian—who is actively involved in meeting the needs of society.

There are two things I want you to notice from my comments above: (1) Pretribulationists are not the only Christians who are heavenly minded. Great Christian leaders such as C.S. Lewis and J.I. Packer were and are also heavenly minded. If critics target pretribulationists for being heavenly minded, then, to be consistent, shouldn't Lewis and Packer also be targeted? Don't get me wrong. I do not wish for that to happen. I'm just saying it is unfair to level charges against pretribulationists alone when others clearly hold to the same view. (2) Those of us who are heavenly minded—whether pretribulationists or not—believe that such a mindset is biblical. One of many passages that speaks to this issue is Colossians 3:1-2: "Seek the things that are above...Set your minds on things that are above." The apostle Paul, who wrote these words, was certainly heavenly minded. Jesus Himself spoke of being heavenly minded when He urged His followers, "Lay up for yourselves treasures in heaven, where neither moth nor rust destroys and where thieves do not break in and steal. For where your treasure is, there your heart will be also" (Matthew 6:20-21).

• • •

Critics sometimes claim that pretribulationists cherry-pick verses they imagine support their view while completely ignoring the many other passages of Scripture that contradict their view. I believe this claim is fallacious. Pretrib scholars have consistently wrestled with verses that seem to challenge pretribulationism. I have wrestled with many of these verses in my books on prophecy.

Please allow me to give you an example. In Matthew 24:40-41, Jesus said, "Two men will be in the field; one will be taken and one left. Two women will be grinding at the mill; one will be taken and one left." The context of these verses is the "coming of the Son of Man," or the second coming (verse 39). This is a challenging passage for pretribulationists. At first glance, it appears to support a rapture that takes place in conjunction with the second coming. The verse is often cited as supportive evidence for posttribulationism.

However, a parallel passage for Matthew 24:40-41 is Luke 17:34-37, where Jesus shows that those who are "taken" are taken not in the rapture but *in judgment.* In this passage, Jesus informs His followers: "'I tell you, in that night there will be two in one bed. One will be taken and the other left. There will be two women grinding together. One will be taken and the other left.' And they said to him, 'Where, Lord?' He said to them, 'Where the corpse is, there the vultures will gather.'" So, where will they be taken? To a place where vultures feed upon dead corpses. In other words, these people will be taken away *in judgment*. Hence, Matthew 24:37-40 does not support a posttribulational rapture after all. It merely supports the idea of judgment following the second coming. Now, the very fact that pretribulationists deal with this challenging verse proves they are not cherry-picking, as charged.

Another example relates to the fact that there will be Christians who live during the tribulation period, an idea that might seem to argue against a pretribulational rapture. In other words, if Christians are removed from earth *before* the tribulation period, then why does Scripture indicate there are Christians on earth *during* the tribulation period? The primary passage in Scripture that speaks of saints during the tribulation period is Revelation 7:9-17. If pretribulationists were cherry-picking, they would ignore this passage. But pretribs do not ignore it. They explain that these are people who *become* Christians during the tribulation period, long after the rapture has occurred. They likely become Christians as a result of the ministries of the two prophetic witnesses in Revelation 11 (who perform incredible miracles) and the 144,000 Jewish witnesses in Revelation 7 and 14. Now, again, the very fact that pretribulationists deal with this issue proves they are not cherry-picking, as charged.

In the interest of fairness, pretribulationists can just as easily charge that posttribulationists are cherry-picking verses they imagine support their view while completely ignoring the many other passages of Scripture that contradict their view. An example relates to the judgment of the nations in Matthew 25:31-46. The nations mentioned in this passage are comprised of the sheep and the goats, representing the saved and the lost among the Gentiles. According to Matthew 25:32, they are intermingled and require separation by a special judgment. They are judged based upon how they treat Christ's "brothers." Who are these brothers? It is likely that they are the 144,000 Jews mentioned in Revelation 7, Christ's Jewish brothers who bear witness of Him during the tribulation.

These Jewish witnesses will find it difficult to buy food during the tribulation period because they refused to receive the mark of the beast (Revelation 13:16-17). Only true believers in the Lord will be willing to jeopardize their lives by extending hospitality to the messengers. These "sheep" (believers) who treat the brothers (the 144,000) well will enter Christ's millennial kingdom. The goats (unbelievers), by contrast, will go to eternal punishment.

Now, here is the problem for posttribulationism. According to posttribulationists, *all* Christians are raptured after the tribulation period. This would demand that both the sheep and the brothers be among those who will be raptured and they will meet Christ up in the air. Matthew 25:32 does not mesh with such a posttrib rapture: "Before [Jesus] will be gathered all the nations, and he will separate people one from another as a shepherd separates the sheep from the goats." The problem is that the sheep (along with the brothers) have just been "separated" from the goats by the rapture. The sheep meet Christ in the air and are no longer available to be "gathered" on the earth to take part in the judgment of the nations. Hence, this judgment of the sheep and goats poses an immense problem for posttribulationism. It poses no problem for pretribulationism. Posttribulationists—*almost without exception*—ignore this problematic passage. Some might say this is cherry-picking.

* * *

"Every time somebody burps in the Middle East," pretribs jump up and down, thinking a new prophecy has been fulfilled. This is the gist of an actual statement from a preterist. The idea is that pretribulationists find fulfillments of prophecy just about everywhere, thereby showing that they lack prophetic discernment.

This is another example of an *argumentum ad hominem*. If a critic wanted to address the substance of the issue, he would say something like this: "Pretribs see too many things as fulfillments of prophecy."

Instead, the critic claimed, "Every time somebody burps in the Middle East," pretribs jump up and down, thinking a new prophecy has been fulfilled. Wording it this way undermines the character of pretribs, making them look silly. Such wording illustrates the darker side of prophecy under siege.

If we can get past the *ad hominem* language, I think there is a good point for us to be aware of. There are indeed some Christians who see too many "signs of the times." But I'm not aware of any *theologically trained* pretribulationists—those with legitimate theological degrees—who go overboard with the signs of the times. I'm talking about people like the late Norman Geisler, the late Ed Hindson, John Ankerberg, Wayne House, Mark Hitchcock, Charles Swindoll, David Jeremiah, Thomas Ice, Jeff Kinley, and Todd Hampson.

People who succumb to this problem face an interpretive dilemma: "The problem is that when everything becomes a sign, then nothing is a sign."[11] People can categorize so many things in the world as "signs" that signs end up losing their significance. Pretrib leaders need to train pretrib laypeople to watch out for this danger.

The best way to avoid interpreting too many things as a sign is to thoroughly know our Bible—specifically, what the Bible teaches about prophecy. Once we thoroughly understand the prophetic teachings of the Bible, it is easier for us to watch for *legitimate* correlations in the world.

I am compelled to mention that not only are there some who go overboard with the signs of the times, there are also others—in competing prophetic schools of thought—who *ignore* the signs of the times. Preterists, in particular, see *no* signs of the times being fulfilled today. This, in my thinking, is an extremely unbalanced viewpoint, and is far more problematic than seeing too many signs of the times. (I will address preterism in chapters 5, 6, 7, and 8.)

• • •

Some critics allege that the teaching of an any-moment rapture is nothing but a scare tactic to pressure people into becoming believers before the event occurs. The idea is, "Get in while there is yet time." This claim is false. In fact, it is nonsense. In my decades of ministry, I have never witnessed a single example either among pretrib leaders or pretrib laypeople of attempting to scare someone into God's kingdom by advocating an any-moment rapture. This charge is just as nonsensical as the claim, "Preterism provides a license to sin, given that all the judgments of Revelation and Matthew 24–25 relate to the past and not the future. We don't have to worry about such judgments." Preterists would rightly be offended by this ridiculous statement, just as pretribulationists are offended by the scare tactic claim.

Let's do the right thing and keep the discussion focused on Scripture, shall we?

• • •

A common criticism of pretribulationists is that they often set dates for the rapture and other end-times events, and—as expected—these dates have never materialized. The truth is that hardly any pretrib leaders have set dates for the rapture and other prophetic events. Unfortunately, the few people who have set dates have received phenomenal national publicity, which has given a bad name to the rest of us.

Previously in this book, I noted that Edgar C. Whisenant wrote *88 Reasons Why the Rapture Will Be in 1988.* Harold Camping likewise wrote a book titled *1994?* that claimed the rapture would occur in September 1994. But such individuals are the exception and not the rule. Most pretrib leaders are thoughtful and responsible in their approach to prophecy. On the internet, one can find a plethora of responsible pretribulationists at the Pretrib Research Center. (A simple internet search will take you to this organization's website.)

Contrary to what critics would have you believe, quite a number of pretribulationists have warned other Christians *against* setting dates for end-times events. I count myself in this group. For example, in my book *Bible Prophecy Answer Book* (Harvest House Publishers), I offer eight reasons Christians should avoid date-setting:

1. First, date-setters tend to be sensationalistic, and sensationalism is unbefitting to a Christian. Christ calls His followers to live soberly and alertly as they await His coming (Mark 13:32-37).

2. Throughout the past 2,000 years, the track record of those who have set specific dates for end-times events has been 100 percent wrong. Doomsday predictions are little more than a history of dashed expectations.

3. Those who succumb to date-setting may end up making harmful decisions for their lives. Selling one's possessions and heading for the mountains, purchasing bomb shelters, stockpiling weapons, stopping education, and leaving family and friends—these are destructive actions.

4. Christians who succumb to date-setting—for example, by expecting the rapture to occur by a specific date—may damage their faith in the Bible (especially prophetic sections) when their expectations fail.

5. Related to this, Christians who succumb to date-setting may damage the faith of new or immature believers when predicted events fail to materialize.

6. If one loses confidence in the prophetic portions of Scripture, Bible prophecy ceases to be a motivation for purity and holiness (see Titus 2:11-14).

7. Christians who get caught up in date-setting can damage the cause of Christ. Humanists and atheists enjoy scorning

Christians who have put stock in end-times predictions—especially when specific dates have been attached to specific events. Why give ammunition to the enemies of Christianity?

8. The timing of end-times events is in God's hands, and we haven't been given the precise details (Acts 1:7). As far as the rapture is concerned, it is better to live as if Jesus were coming today and yet prepare for the future as if He were not coming for a long time. This way, we are prepared for time and eternity.

Of course, simply because we are not to set specific dates for end-times events does not mean we cannot be excited about the rapture, which could occur at any moment. Not a single prophecy needs to be fulfilled before the rapture occurs. That is why we call the rapture a "signless event."

Here, then, is what it all comes down to:

DON'T set dates for prophetic events like the rapture. The other prophetic schools of thought are right to criticize this in the very few instances that it occurs.

DO stay excited that the rapture could occur at any moment.

* * *

Some critics claim pretribs are naïve. They say many pretribs believed that the year 2000—with the "new millennium"—would bring about "the end." Many pretribs also thought the "blood moons" indicated the end was near. The same is true regarding COVID-19 (an "end-times plague"). The rapture is said to be just one more naïve viewpoint.

For the record, I am not personally aware of any pretribulationist leader who believed or promoted the idea that the year 2000 would bring about "the end." (And I know a lot of pretrib leaders.) On the contrary, responsible pretrib leaders warned against the idea. I count myself in this group. Back in 1990, I wrote an article titled "Millennial Madness," published in the *Christian Research Journal*. In that article, I warned that millennial madness

> swept across the world at near-epidemic levels just prior
> to AD 1000, and we will no doubt witness much of the
> same as we approach the turn of the second millennium.
> Some are predicting imminent doom, others a glorious
> utopia. Either way, millennial madness is on the rise and
> will almost certainly afflict a significant share of humanity
> over the next decade.[12]

In that article, I provided substantive reasons Christians should not give in to millennial hysteria. Other pretrib leaders—Norman Geisler, Mark Hitchcock, and Ed Hindson, to name a few—also warned people about this.

To be fair, there were undoubtedly many laypeople from *all* the prophetic persuasions—pretribs, posttribs, midtribs, and others—who wondered how the year 2000 might relate to their unique prophetic viewpoints. To target pretribs alone with the charge of naïveté is unfair.

Moreover, I do not think pretribs are naïve simply because they investigated the blood moon phenomena. After all, Scripture prophetically warns in Joel 2:31, "The sun shall be turned to darkness, and the moon to blood, before the great and awesome day of the LORD comes" (compare with Acts 2:20). Christians are simply measuring current events against the prophetic scriptures to ascertain whether there is a legitimate correlation.

The same is true regarding COVID-19. In Luke 21:11, Jesus prophetically warned about "pestilences" in the end times. Revelation 6:8 speaks of how more than a fourth of earth's population will die partially due to pestilence. Revelation 16:2 speaks of "harmful and painful sores" that will come upon people during the tribulation period.

This may indicate the spread of a viral contagion. My point is that if the prophetic scriptures warn of pestilences in the end times, it is not naïve to wonder if COVID-19 might be setting the stage for these pestilences during the tribulation period.

As for the rapture being another example of a naïve viewpoint, I think the scriptural evidence provided in this book sufficiently debunks this silly claim.

• • •

Anti-pretrib critics point out that one-fourth of all Christian pastors reject pretribulationism. This reportedly says something bad about pretribulationism.

Christian pastors have different views on all kinds of issues, including spiritual gifts like healing and speaking in tongues, divorce and remarriage, the nature of biblical inerrancy, the nature of sanctification, original sin and the fall, the extent of the atonement, God and the problem of evil, the role of women in the church, forms of church government, the use of musical instruments in church, traditional hymns versus contemporary Christian music, covenant theology versus dispensationalism, the "days" of Genesis 1, the significance of the Lord's Supper, eternal punishment, water baptism, eternal security, the relationship of Israel and the church, Christianity and science, faith and reason, and many other important issues!

The fact that one-fourth of pastors reject a pretribulational rapture is neither surprising nor significant. It is not surprising because prophecy debates have been commonplace for a long time. It is not significant because the truthfulness of a view is based not on how many people hold to it, but on what the Bible teaches. The Bible is our sole barometer of truth. We must test all teachings against Scripture (Acts 17:11; 1 Thessalonians 5:21).

As a matter of observation, it is unwise to engage in arguments such as "one-fourth of pastors reject pretribulationism." I say this because a poll of pastors shows that 36 percent of them—"the largest proportion by far"—align themselves with pretribulationism. Only 18 percent hold to posttribulationism. The other prophetic schools of thought had far lower percentages of supporters. Hence, statistically speaking, pretribulationism is the most popular of the bunch![13]

• • •

As I close this chapter, allow me to emphasize that Jesus used Scripture as the final court of appeal in every matter under dispute. Jesus affirmed the Bible's divine inspiration (Matthew 22:43), its indestructibility (Matthew 5:17-18), its infallibility (John 10:35), its ultimate authority (Matthew 4:4, 7, 10), its historicity (Matthew 12:40; 24:37), its scientific accuracy (Matthew 19:2-5), and its factual inerrancy (Matthew 22:29; John 17:17).

To the Sadducees, Jesus said: "You are in error because you do not know the Scriptures or the power of God" (Matthew 22:29 NIV). He told some Pharisees that they invalidated the Word of God by their human tradition, which had been handed down by mere men (Mark 7:13). Jesus informed them, "Neglecting the commandment of God, you hold to the tradition of men" (Mark 7:8 NASB). To the devil, Jesus consistently responded, "It is written…" (Matthew 4:4-10).

Should we not be following Jesus' lead?

Should we not make our primary concern what Scripture teaches instead of attacking the character of other Christians?

• • •

In the next chapter, we will shift our attention to claims about Israel and the church. Maintaining a distinction between these two entities is critical to pretribulational theology.

4

OUT WITH ISRAEL, IN WITH THE CHURCH

One Bible verse that was drilled into my mind as a seminary student in the early 1980s was 2 Timothy 2:15. This verse is all about "rightly handling the word of truth." It is instructive to consult a variety of Bible translations on this verse. The Expanded Bible says that each of us should be a worker "who uses the true teaching in the right way [correctly handles the true message/word of truth; or holds carefully to the true message/word of truth]." The Amplified Bible says that each of us should be "a workman who has no cause to be ashamed, correctly analyzing and accurately dividing [rightly handling and skillfully teaching] the Word of Truth." The New English Translation Bible puts it more simply, affirming that we should be "teaching the message of truth accurately." The King James Version says we should be "rightly dividing the word of truth."

It is critically important to "rightly divide" Israel and the church. Failing to do so will lead one far astray in interpreting prophecy. God has made certain prophetic promises to Israel and other prophetic promises to the church. Many today—advocates of what is called "replacement theology"—claim the church is a continuation of Old Testament Israel. They say the church is the "new Israel" or "spiritual Israel." This view holds that "Israel's sin and failure caused God to set aside national Israel completely and permanently and replace it with the church. The promises given to Israel in the Old Testament have been transferred over to the church."[1] So, the church *replaces* Israel as the people of God. Given this, we might say that Israel's place in Bible prophecy is under siege by replacement theologians.

Following are some of the primary arguments offered in support of the idea that the church is the new Israel.

• • •

Proponents of replacement theology typically claim that the biblical covenants God made with Israel were conditional. They reason that because Israel did not live up to the covenant stipulations, there is no biblical basis for a future for national Israel in prophecy. This means there is no prophetic significance to the rebirth of Israel as a nation in 1948. It also means that God will not be fulfilling promises made to Israel in the Abrahamic and Davidic covenants in the future millennial kingdom.

Let's pause a moment to consider the backdrop of the biblical covenants. There were two kinds of covenants in Bible times— conditional and unconditional. A *conditional* covenant is a covenant with an "if" attached. Conditions were required for the promises to be fulfilled. A conditional covenant between God and human beings required that human beings meet certain conditions before God was obligated to fulfill what He promised. Such a covenant might be as simple as this: "Obey Me [*condition*], and I will bless you [*promise*]." If God's people did not meet the conditions, God was under no obligation to fulfill His promises.

An *unconditional* covenant, by contrast, did not depend on conditions for its fulfillment—there were no "ifs" attached. An unconditional covenant between God and human beings involved God's firm and inviolable promises apart from any merit (or lack thereof) of the human beings to whom God made the promises. This type of covenant is also known as a *unilateral covenant* because only one party (God) makes the promises. Others prefer the term *one-sided covenant* or *divine commitment covenant.*

Contrary to the claims of those in the replacement camp, the Abrahamic covenant is an unconditional covenant. We know this to be true because, according to ancient custom, the two parties of a conditional covenant would divide an animal into two equal parts and then walk between the two parts, showing that each was responsible for fulfilling the obligations of the covenant (Jeremiah 34:18-19). However, with the Abrahamic covenant, God alone passed between the parts after He put Abraham into a deep sleep (Genesis 15:12, 17). This proves that God made unconditional promises to Abraham in this covenant. Hence, the land promises to Israel in this covenant are unconditional and will find ultimate fulfillment in the future millennial kingdom when Israel comes into full possession of the land.

Even far after the time of Abraham, many Bible verses continue to confirm the land promises God made to Abraham (see Isaiah 60:21; Jeremiah 24:6; 30:18; 32:37-38; 33:6-9; Ezekiel 28:25-26; 34:11-12; 36:24-26; 39:28; Hosea 3:4-5; Micah 2:12; 4:6-7; Amos 9:14-15; Zephaniah 3:20; Zechariah 8:7-8). Every Old Testament prophet except Jonah speaks of a permanent return to the land of Israel by the Jews. This points to the unconditional nature of the Abrahamic covenant.

The Davidic covenant, too, is an unconditional covenant. We know this because long after the time of David, the angel Gabriel appeared to Mary before Jesus' birth and informed her about her child: "The Lord God will give to him the *throne* of his father David, and he will reign over the *house* of Jacob forever, and of his *kingdom* there will be no end" (Luke 1:32-33, emphasis added). Notice the three significant words in this passage—*throne, house,* and *kingdom.* These words are

derived directly from God's promise to David in the Davidic covenant: "I will raise up your offspring after you, who shall come from
your body, and I will establish his *kingdom*. He shall build a *house*
for my name, and I will establish the *throne* of his kingdom forever"
(2 Samuel 7:12-13, emphasis added). Gabriel's words must have immediately brought these Old Testament promises to mind for Mary, a
devout young Jew. Gabriel's words were a clear announcement that
the babe in her womb would fulfill the Davidic covenant. Her baby
would one day rule on the throne of David in the future kingdom as
the divine Messiah. Gabriel's words were full of prophetic anticipation.

In Old Testament times, God Himself confirmed His absolute
and irrevocable intention to fulfill the promises He made to David,
even in the face of Israel's unfaithfulness:

> If they do not obey my decrees and fail to keep my
> commands, then I will punish their sin with the rod,
> and their disobedience with beating. But I will never stop
> loving him nor fail to keep my promise to him. No, I will
> not break my covenant; I will not take back a single word
> I said. I have sworn an oath to David, and in my holiness
> I cannot lie: His dynasty will go on forever; his kingdom
> will endure as the sun (Psalm 89:31-36 NLT).

I am reminded of the apostle Paul's words about God: "If we are
faithless, he remains faithful—for he cannot deny himself" (2 Timothy 2:13).

Contrary to the claims of replacement theologians, the prophetic
promises in the unconditional Abrahamic and Davidic covenants
indicate that God has a plan for Israel. The Abrahamic covenant
makes specific land promises to Israel, while the Davidic covenant
indicates Christ will reign on the throne of David. Both covenant
promises will be fulfilled during Christ's future millennial kingdom.

At present, however, Israel is in a state of spiritual blindness. The backdrop is that the Davidic kingdom (2 Samuel 7:8-14) had been offered to the Jewish people by Jesus in the first century (Matthew 11–12). However, the Jewish leaders rejected Jesus and claimed He performed miracles using the power of Satan. This was a vile accusation. Jesus did miracles in the power of the Holy Spirit, but the Jewish leaders insisted He was doing miracles in the power of the *un*holy spirit—Satan. This accusation constituted a decisive turning away from Jesus as the Jewish Messiah. God therefore inflicted judicial blindness and hardening upon Israel as a divine judgment (Romans 11:25).

This, in turn, resulted in a delay of the fulfillment of God's kingdom promises to Israel. These promises have now been postponed until Christ's future millennial kingdom, which will follow the second coming (Matthew 11–12).

God will not lift this judicial blindness until the end of the tribulation period. God's goal is to make the Jews jealous of His offer of salvation. He has done this by opening the gospel to the Gentiles ever since the first century AD (Romans 11:11). With the Jews no longer in the special place of God's blessing—and with Gentiles now experiencing God's salvation—God is slowly but surely moving the Jews toward repentance. At the end of the tribulation period, the blindness of the Jews will be lifted, and a Jewish remnant will repent and turn to Jesus as their Messiah (verse 25).

Meanwhile, God has a different purpose for the church during this current age. Members of the church are called to be Christ's witnesses (Luke 24:45-49; Acts 1:7-8), build up the body of Christ (Ephesians 4:11-13), do good to all people (Galatians 6:10; Titus 3:14), exercise spiritual gifts (Romans 12:6-8), financially support God's work (1 Corinthians 16:1-3), help brothers and sisters in need (1 John 3:16-18), love each other (Hebrews 13:1-3, 16), make disciples of all nations (Matthew 28:19-20), offer hospitality to each other (1 Peter 4:9-11), and preach the Word of God (Mark 16:15-16; 1 Timothy 4:6, 13). Many local churches may fail in one or more of these tasks, but these tasks comprise God's calling on the church.

• • •

Proponents of replacement theology assert that the church is the new Israel or spiritual Israel that has permanently replaced or super- seded Israel as the people of God. They claim that God has already fulfilled all His promises to ancient Israel and that the church is the only people of God today. Replacement theologians often criticize pretribulationists for their view that Scripture distinguishes between Israel and the church, and their view that God has different prophetic plans for each. They say there is no biblical basis for such a distinction.

Following is the "biblical basis" for distinguishing Israel and the church that replacement theologians seem to have overlooked:

1. The New Testament portrays the church as being distinct from Israel. For example, in 1 Corinthians 10:32 we are exhorted: "Give no offense to Jews or to Greeks or to the church of God." The "Jews" are portrayed as distinct from "the church of God" in this verse. Moreover, Israel and the church are viewed as distinct throughout the book of Acts, where the word *Israel* is used 20 times, and the word *church* 19 times. New Testament scholar S. Lewis Johnson notes that "the usage of the terms *Israel* and the *church* in the early chapters of the book of Acts is in complete harmony, for Israel exists there alongside the newly formed church, and the two entities are kept separate in terminology."[2] We can also observe that the term *Israel* "is used seventy-three times in the New Testament, and in each occurrence it refers to ethnic Israel, either the nation as a whole or believing Jews within the nation."[3] This means that during New Testament

times, the church was not considered to be the new Israel or spiritual Israel. Israel and the church were viewed as distinct from each other. This means replacement theology is without a leg to stand on.

2. The consistent use of the historical-grammatical method in Bible interpretation demands that the unconditional land and throne promises of the Abrahamic and Davidic covenants be literally fulfilled in Israel alone, and not the church (Genesis 12:1-3; 15:18-21; 17:21; 35:10-12; 2 Samuel 7:12ff.). Let's remember that the historical-grammatical method enables us to understand all the attributes of God, the absolute deity of Jesus Christ, the deity and personhood of the Holy Spirit, the doctrine of humankind's fall into sin, the gospel of salvation by grace through faith, a future judgment for humankind, and an afterlife involving heaven for the saved and hell for the unsaved. *The same historical-grammatical method reveals a distinction in Scripture between Israel and the church, and the future fulfillment of the Abrahamic and Davidic covenants in Israel in the millennial kingdom.* We cannot use the historical-grammatical method when convenient to our theological position and then switch to allegory when it isn't convenient. We must *consistently* use the historical-grammatical method. When we do so, the distinction between Israel and the church remains intact.

3. The New Testament reveals that God still has a plan for national Israel. The apostle Paul indicated national Israel would one day repent and then be restored before Christ returns in the end times (Romans 11:1-2, 29). A remnant of the Jews will become followers of Jesus the Messiah. The restoration of Israel will include the confession of

Israel's national sin (Leviticus 26:40-42; Jeremiah 3:11-
18; Hosea 5:15), after which Israel will be saved, fulfilling
Paul's prophecy in Romans 11:25-27. In dire threat at Armageddon (the antichrist will be poised to attack), Israel will
plead for their newly found Messiah to return and deliver
them—they will "mourn for him, as one mourns for an
only child" (Zechariah 12:10; see also Matthew 23:37-39;
Isaiah 53:1-9)—at which point their deliverance will surely
come (see Romans 10:13-14. These saved Jews will then
be invited into Christ's millennial kingdom, and they will
experience the blessings promised in the Abrahamic and
Davidic covenants.

These theological facts demonstrate that the church is not a new
Israel or spiritual Israel. The church and Israel are portrayed as distinct in the New Testament, and God has different prophetic plans
for each. However, there are several Bible passages—Joshua 21:43-45;
Galatians 3:29; 6:16; and Philippians 3:3—that replacement theologians often cite to support their view. It is to these passages that we
now turn our attention.

• • •

Proponents of replacement theology say that Joshua 21:43-45
proves that the church supersedes Israel, for all of God's promises
to Israel have already been fulfilled in the past. This passage affirms:

The LORD gave to Israel all the land that he swore to give
to their fathers. And they took possession of it, and they
settled there. And the LORD gave them rest on every side
just as he had sworn to their fathers. Not one of all their
enemies had withstood them, for the LORD had given all
their enemies into their hands. Not one word of all the

good promises that the LORD had made to the house of Israel had failed; all came to pass.

Proponents of replacement theology say that because God gave the Israelites the land, God's land promises to Israel are entirely fulfilled. After all, the text tells us that "not one word of all the good promises that the LORD had made to the house of Israel had failed; all came to pass." Replacement theologians thus reason that the modern state of Israel has no legitimate biblical basis. The existence of Israel today is allegedly not a fulfillment of Bible prophecy because all the land promises were fulfilled in the past.

Several pertinent points refute this understanding of Joshua 21:43-45. Foundationally, while God fulfilled His part in giving the Israelites the Promised Land, Israel failed to fully possess what God promised the nation. They failed to dispossess all the Canaanites, even though the gift of land had been made by God. It was there for the taking. God had faithfully done for Israel what He promised. Israel, by contrast, was not completely faithful. The Lord had not failed in His gift of the land to Israel, but Israel failed to fully "receive" that gift by conquering and entering all the land.

The *Believer's Bible Commentary* puts it this way:

> There were still enemies within the land; not all the Canaanites had been destroyed. But that was not God's fault; He fulfilled His promise by defeating every foe against which the Israelites fought. If there were still undefeated foes and pockets of resistance, it was because Israel did not claim God's promise.[4]

The claim that there are no further land promises to be fulfilled for Israel is proven false by the many prophecies written far after the time of Joshua that speak of Israel possessing the land in the future, in fulfillment of God's covenant with Abraham (see for example: Isaiah 60:18, 21; Jeremiah 23:6; 24:5-6; 30:18; 31:31-34; 32:37-40; 33:6-9; Ezekiel 28:25-26; 34:11-12; 36:24-26; 37; 39:28; Hosea 3:4-5; Joel 2:18-29; Amos 9:14-15; Micah 2:12; 4:6-7; Zephaniah 3:19-20; Zechariah 8:7-8; 13:8-9). This makes it impossible that God's land promises to Abraham were completely fulfilled in Joshua 21:43-45.

We can also observe that although Israel possessed some of the land during the time of Joshua, *it was later dispossessed*. The Abrahamic covenant, however, promised Israel that she would possess the land *forever* (Genesis 17:8). This alone renders the replacement interpretation of Joshua 21:43-45 impossible. This *never-ending* possession of the land will not take place until the future millennial kingdom.

• • •

Proponents of replacement theology say that Galatians 3:29 proves that their view is correct. In this verse, the apostle Paul said, "If you are Christ's, then you are Abraham's offspring, heirs according to promise." This must mean the church is the new Israel since the church is "Abraham's offspring."

This interpretation is incorrect for the following reasons:

1. Scripture interprets scripture. This principle means that if we interpret one portion of Scripture in such a way that it contradicts another portion of Scripture, we have misinterpreted one of those passages. The claim that Galatians 3:29 establishes replacement theology is proven false because the same apostle Paul who wrote this verse also wrote Romans 9–11, where he said that God still has a future plan for ethnic Israel as distinct from the church. A remnant of Israel—at the end of the tribulation period—will exercise faith in Jesus the Messiah and become saved. The remnant will then be invited into Christ's millennial kingdom.

2. Properly understood, Galatians 3:29 does not mean that Christians become Jews, but they become spiritual descendants of Abraham and become beneficiaries of some of God's promises to him. We are his "spiritual children" because we followed his pattern of faith. Like Abraham, *we are justified by faith.* Once justified by faith, believers benefit from some of the promises made to Abraham. Bible expositor Thomas Constable explains that "those joined to Christ by faith become spiritual descendants of Abraham and beneficiaries of some of God's promises to him…God promised some things to all the physical descendants of Abraham (e.g., Gen. 12:1-3, 7). He promised other things to the believers within that group (e.g., Rom. 9:6, 8). He promised still other things to the spiritual seed of Abraham who are not Jews (e.g., Gal. 3:6-9). Failure to distinguish these groups and the promises given to each has resulted in much confusion."[5] So, again, having been justified by faith, believers become spiritual recipients of some of the promises made to Abraham. Seen in this light, Galatians 3:29 does not support replacement theology. The church is not the new Israel.

• • •

Proponents of replacement theology say that Philippians 3:3 proves the church is the new Israel. After all, believers in Christ are called "the circumcision."

The problem with this interpretation is that the apostle Paul was referring not to physical circumcision (as practiced by the Jews) but to the spiritual circumcision of the heart that occurs when a person trusts in Christ for salvation. "Paul was referring to the circumcision of the heart that happens when a person trusts in Jesus Christ…The true circumcision refers to believers in the church, not that the church is the 'new Israel.'"[6] The claim that this verse proves the church is the new Israel is *eisegesis* (reading a meaning into the text) as opposed to *exegesis* (drawing the meaning out of the text).

• • •

Replacement theologians say Galatians 6:16 proves that the church is the new Israel. After all, the apostle Paul refers to "the Israel of God" in this verse.

This verse does not mean the church is the new Israel. The verse does not deny that the church and Israel remain distinct (see 1 Corinthians 10:32; Romans 9–11). Rather, Paul is here referring to *saved Jews*—Jews who have trusted in Jesus Christ for salvation. An example of "the Israel of God" is the apostle Paul, a Jew who trusted in Christ on the road to Damascus.

How do saved Jews relate to the church? If an individual Jew places faith in Christ in the current church age, that Jew is absorbed into the body of Christ, becoming part of the church (see Romans 10:12-13; Galatians 3:28). But God still has a future prophetic plan for national Israel (Romans 9–11).

New Testament scholar F.F. Bruce, in his book *The Epistle to the Galatians,* commented that "for all his demoting of the law and the customs, Paul held good hope of the ultimate blessing of Israel."[7] Because Paul spoke of God's ultimate blessing of Israel—a blessing involving the salvation of a remnant of the Jews in the tribulation period—the church cannot be viewed as the new Israel. Israel and the church remain distinct in God's prophetic plan.

• • •

We must never forget that God is a promise keeper. Numbers 23:19 asserts, "God is not man, that he should lie, or a son of man, that he should change his mind. Has he said, and will he not do it? Or has he spoken, and will he not fulfill it?" Prior to his death, an aged Joshua declared, "Now I am about to go the way of all the earth, and you know in your hearts and souls, all of you, that not one word has failed of all the good things that the LORD your God promised concerning you. All have come to pass for you; not one of them has failed" (Joshua 23:14). Solomon later proclaimed: "Blessed be the LORD who has given rest to his people Israel, according to all that he promised. Not one word has failed of all his good promise, which he spoke by Moses his servant" (1 Kings 8:56; see also Joshua 21:45). God truly is faithful! And because of that, *He will honor the Abrahamic and Davidic covenants with His people Israel.*

The apostle Paul was absolutely certain of this. Indeed, he forcefully emphasized that God will not cast away or reject His people, Israel. He said, "I ask, then, has God rejected his people [Israel]? By no means!" (Romans 11:1). The King James Version translates it, "I say then, Hath God cast away his people? God forbid." The New King James Version puts it, "I say then, has God cast away His people? Certainly not!" The New American Standard Version translates it, "I say then, God has not rejected His people, has He? Far from it!" The Expanded Bible translates it, "So I ask: Did God throw out [cast away; reject] his people? No [Absolutely not; May it never be]." So, contrary to proponents of replacement theology, God has not rejected Israel, nor has He forgotten His future plans for Israel. Paul's unbending attitude is: *By no means! God forbid. Certainly not. Far from it. Absolutely not. May it never be.*

● ● ●

I close with an expression of sorrow that replacement theology has done much damage to the cause of Israel. Because of this theology, many Christians have abandoned support for Israel and her right to stay in the land. Based on the Abrahamic covenant—an unconditional covenant—I believe the land unconditionally belongs to Israel. I pray the United States will remain committed to protecting Israel against its many enemies.

Tragically, replacement theology has been a motivation for at least some people to engage in anti-Semitism. Prophecy expert Thomas Ice notes that "wherever replacement theology has flourished, the Jews have had to run for cover."[8] Christians therefore ought to give cautious consideration to this debate.

• • •

We will begin our examination of the preterist view of prophecy in the next chapter.

5

EXAMINING THE PRETERIST CASE FOR AN EARLY DATE OF REVELATION

I often joined Hank Hanegraaff on the national *Bible Answer Man* radio broadcast in the late 1980s and early 1990s—generally, four out of the five shows per week. It is hard to believe that more than three decades have passed since then.

Back in those days, Hank had not quite decided about where he stood on eschatology. He has since become an advocate of what he calls "exegetical eschatology." A perusal of his books reveals that his exegetical eschatology bears a striking resemblance to partial preterism—a fact recognized by Dr. Norman L. Geisler, Dr. Thomas A. Howe, Dr. Mark Hitchcock, and others.

The word *preterism* derives from the Latin *preter*, meaning "past." According to this view, the prophecies in the book of Revelation (especially chapters 6–18) and those in Christ's Olivet Discourse (Matthew 24–25) have already been fulfilled. Specifically, the prophecies were fulfilled in AD 70 when General Titus and his Roman warriors

overran Jerusalem and destroyed the Jewish temple. Hence, the book
of Revelation does not deal with the future. As Thomas Ice humor-
ously put it, "The preterist view does not view Bible prophecy as
'things to come,' but rather as 'things that came.'"[1]

There are two forms of preterism: (1) Partial preterism is represented by modern writers such as R.C. Sproul, Hank Hanegraaff,
and Gary DeMar. While they believe the literal resurrection and second coming of Christ are yet future, they say the other prophecies
in Revelation and Matthew 24–25 were fulfilled when Jerusalem fell
in AD 70. (2) Full preterism goes so far as to say that *all* New Testament predictions were fulfilled in the past, including those of the
resurrection and the second coming.

The primary components of preterism include:

- God has no prophetic plan for national Israel.

- The great harlot of Revelation was apostate Jerusalem.

- The great tribulation refers to the fall of Jerusalem in AD 70.

- The beast of Revelation was the Roman emperor Nero.

- The second coming (in full preterism) is Christ's coming in
  judgment against Israel through the Roman army in AD 70.

- The millennial kingdom was the kingdom of Jesus that was
  established at His first coming.

- The New Jerusalem is the church.

In the present chapter, I will briefly and selectively examine the
preterist case for an early date of the book of Revelation. Such selec-
tivity is required given the space restraints in this short book.

• • •

Preterists view the book of Revelation primarily as a prophecy of the destruction of Jerusalem by the Romans in AD 70 and the 42 months (three-and-a-half years) leading up to that destruction.[2] This means the book of Revelation had to be written before this time—in the mid-60s AD. Preterism depends entirely on an early date for the book of Revelation. Strong evidence for a late date for Revelation—for example, in the 90s AD—would deal a death blow to preterism.[3] Preterist Kenneth Gentry concedes this is true: "If it could be demonstrated that Revelation were written 25 years after the fall of Jerusalem, [then preterist David] Chilton's entire labor would go up in smoke."[4] Gentry is here referring to fellow preterist David Chilton's commentary on Revelation, titled *The Days of Vengeance: An Exposition of the Book of Revelation.*

Preterists set forth several arguments that they think support an early date for Revelation. For example, since John refers to Jerusalem's temple in Revelation 11:1-2, that temple must have been still standing at the time of the writing of Revelation. If it was still standing, Revelation must have been written before AD 70, because in AD 70, the Romans destroyed that temple, along with the rest of Jerusalem.[5]

Futurists respond that in the book of Revelation, John sets forth a vision about *future* things. John is mystically transported to the future in a vision and speaks about future events that will one day unfold (see Revelation 1:10, 19; 4:1). Pretribulationist Thomas Ice notes that the word *saw* "occurs 49 times in 46 verses in Revelation because John is witnessing future events."[6] Revelation 11:1-2 is therefore prophetic: "It ought to be obvious to everyone that a prophetic passage about the temple does not require the actual physical existence of a temple in Jerusalem."[7] John saw a vision of the future. That being so, the reference to the temple in Revelation 11:1-2 does not support an early date for Revelation.

Paul Benware and Charles C. Ryrie, in their book *Understanding End Times Prophecy*, note the biblical precedent for the idea that a reference to a temple by a spokesman for God does not require the actual existence of a temple:

> When Daniel (in Babylon after 586 BC) wrote prophetically about a temple (e.g., Dan. 9:27 and 12:11), *no temple existed.* When Ezekiel was told to measure the temple and write extensively about it (Ezek. 40–48), the temple had been destroyed over a decade earlier *and did not exist.* In Revelation 11, John is simply instructed to measure the temple in his vision, and this does not require the existence of the Jerusalem temple.[8]

If both Daniel and Ezekiel prophesied about a temple when there was no temple in existence in their day, couldn't we expect John to follow the same pattern?[9]

There is another problem with the preterist position. In the same context as John's discussion of the temple is a discussion of the work of the two prophetic witnesses who will minister during the time of the temple. One must ask: When did anything like the ministry of the two witnesses ever occur in the first century while the temple was standing in Jerusalem before AD 70? *The obvious answer is that it didn't.* The entire context of Revelation 11 is yet future.

Further, full preterists who claim that the prophecy of Christ's second coming was fulfilled in Rome's attack on Jerusalem find no support among the ancients. Indeed, if Christ's second coming was fulfilled in the judgment inflicted upon Jerusalem in AD 70, wouldn't John—the author of Revelation—have been clearer on this? He was so very clear on other prophetic issues!

For that matter, wouldn't this idea be reflected in the writings of the church fathers? The early church fathers "never mentioned that Christ's second coming was past. They invariably referred to it as a future event."[10] We can also point to the Didache, an anonymous early Christian treatise that modern scholars date to the first, or, less commonly, the early second century AD. This document proves that the very people who lived through the events of AD 70 regarded the entire Olivet Discourse (including its teachings on the second coming) as a yet unfulfilled prophecy. "There is zero indication from known, extant writings that anyone understood the New Testament prophecies from a preterist's perspective. No early church writings teach that Jesus returned in the first century."[11]

Justin Martyr was born in the first century and certainly knew many believers who lived through the events of AD 70. He wrote just more than 50 years after the destruction of Jerusalem and its temple. He was convinced that prophecies of the tribulation and the return of Christ were *yet future* and had not been fulfilled in AD 70.

In addition, some of the earliest church fathers confirmed a late date of AD 90 or later for the book of Revelation. This includes Irenaeus, who claimed that Revelation was written at the close of the reign of Domitian, which was about AD 96. (For our purposes, when you think of John writing during the reign of Domitian, *think of a late date for Revelation*, since Domitian reigned in the AD 90s. It's important to remember this. It might help to commit the following phrase to memory: DOMITIAN = LATE DATE.)

Irenaeus wrote the following around AD 180:

> We will not, however, incur the risk of pronouncing positively as to the name of Antichrist; for if it were necessary that his name should be distinctly revealed in this present time, it would have been announced by him who beheld the apocalyptic vision. For that was seen not very long time since, but almost in our day, *towards the end of Domitian's reign*.[12]

So that you do not miss the point, John is "him who beheld the

apocalyptic vision" (the book of Revelation). And he did so "towards
the end of Domitian's reign," which would have been around AD 96.
(Remember, DOMITIAN = LATE DATE.) Hence, Irenaeus confirms a late date for the book of Revelation.

Some have questioned the accuracy of Irenaeus on the dating of
Revelation. However, as Benware and Ryrie note, "Grounds for questioning the accuracy of Irenaeus and other early witnesses are purely
subjective...If Irenaeus had been wrong, later witnesses including
Clement of Alexandria, Origen, Victorinus, Eusebius, and Jerome
would have corrected him. Instead, *they confirmed his dating*. Most
modern scholars concur with the confirmation."[13]

Theologian and church historian Philip Schaff says that Irenaeus's testimony of the late Domitian date is "clear and weighty testimony." Scholar J. Richie Smith agrees, "That Irenaeus refers the
Apocalypse to the reign of Domitian is generally admitted by scholars of all shades of opinion."[14] (In case you don't know, the "Apocalypse" is the book of Revelation.)

Victorinus, a bishop of Pettau, died by AD 304, and is therefore
an excellent early witness. He wrote *A Commentary on the Apocalypse of the Blessed John*, in which he affirmed: "When John said these
things, he was on the island of Patmos, condemned to the mines
by Caesar Domitian." He also said: "The time must be understood
in which the written Apocalypse was published, since then reigned
Caesar Domitian."[15]

Eusebius was the bishop of Caesarea and is known as "the father
of church history" due to his classical work *Ecclesiastical History*. Several times in his writings, he dated the book of Revelation to the reign
of Domitian (which was in the AD 90s). His writings are especially
weighty since he had all the early Christian literature at his disposal.
He wrote, "Many were the victims of Domitian's appalling cruelty.
At Rome, great numbers of men distinguished by birth and attain-
ments were for no reason at all banished from the country and their

property confiscated…There is ample evidence that at that time the apostle and evangelist John was still alive, and because of his testimony to the Word of God was sentenced to confinement on the island of Patmos."[16]

Jerome is another powerful witness. In his *Against Jovinianum* (AD 393), he wrote that John was "a prophet, for he saw on the island of Patmos, to which he had been banished by the emperor Domitian as a martyr for the Lord, an Apocalypse containing boundless mysteries of the future." In his *Lives of Illustrious Men*, in which Jerome wrote about John's banishment, he said of John: "In the fourteenth year then after Nero, Domitian having raised a second persecution, [John] was banished to the island of Patmos, and wrote the Apocalypse, on which Justin Martyr and Irenaeus afterward wrote commentaries."[17] So, since DOMITIAN = LATE DATE, Jerome's comment about John writing Revelation following his banishment by emperor Domitian supports a late date for Revelation.

In sum, as scholar R.H. Charles puts it, "The earliest authorities are practically unanimous in assigning the Apocalypse to the last years of Domitian."[18] This means the book of Revelation was written well after AD 70, in the AD 90s. This, in turn, means that the book of Revelation could hardly have been referring to events that would be fulfilled in AD 70.

In further support of this, we can observe that many of the critical events prophesied in the book of Revelation simply did not occur in AD 70. For example, in AD 70 "a third of mankind" was not killed, as predicted in Revelation 9:18. Nor did "every living thing" die "that was in the sea," as predicted in Revelation 16:3. Nor did all the green grass burn up, as predicted in Revelation 8:7. Nor did a third of the sea become blood, as predicted in Revelation 8:8. There are multiple other examples. To explain these and many other such texts, preterists resort to an allegorical interpretation of prophecy.

Strong supportive evidence for a late date of Revelation relates to the seven churches described in Revelation 2–3. Bible scholars have observed that the conditions of the seven churches described in these prophetic verses fit a late date much better than the AD 60s, during which Ephesians, Colossians, and 1 and 2 Timothy were written. For example, the church at Ephesus, as described in Revelation 2:4, had lost its first love—something that was not true of the church in the AD 60s. References to persecution and martyrdom in the churches (for example, Revelation 2:10-13) also reflect a later date. Such persecution and martyrdom were common in the AD 90s and beyond. Further, the Nicolaitans mentioned in Revelation 2:6, 15 were not firmly established until near the end of the first century, thus implying a late date for Revelation. It is also noteworthy that it was not until Domitian's reign that emperor worship, as reflected in the book of Revelation, was instituted.

Apart from the linguistic, theological, and historical arguments in favor of a late date of Revelation, Mark Hitchcock suggests that an early date ultimately makes the book of Revelation irrelevant for most Christians:

> If Revelation was written in AD 65–66 and the events in 1:1–20:6 were fulfilled "soon" in the events of AD 64–70, as partial preterists maintain, then the bulk of the book was already fulfilled before most Christians ever heard or read its contents. By the time the book was written by John on Patmos and was then copied and carried by the messengers of the seven churches and then recopied and widely disseminated, the prophesied events would have already occurred. The powerful prophetic message of the Apocalypse would have been one great anticlimax. By the time most people heard the book's message, the "soon" events of AD 70 would have already occurred. Revelation would have had one of the shortest shelf-lives of any book in history.[19]

For a detailed scholarly defense of the late date of Revelation, I highly recommend Mark Hitchcock's doctoral dissertation at Dallas Theological Seminary, "A Defense of the Domitian Date of the Book of Revelation." A PDF version of the dissertation is free to download at the Pretrib Research Center online.

• • •

Some preterists claim we can determine the date of Revelation simply by identifying the sixth king of Revelation 17:10. This verse speaks of "seven kings, five of whom have fallen, one is, the other has not yet come." Notice that this verse speaks about the past, the present, and the future: There are "seven kings, five of whom have fallen [in the past], one is [in the present], the other has not yet come [he is yet future]." Because we already have accurate dates for the reigns of the Roman emperors, all we have to do, preterists say, is to figure out which emperor was ruling at the time the book of Revelation was written. That would be the sixth emperor, who was ruling *in the present* (from the perspective of the book of Revelation). If it turned out that this sixth emperor happened to be Nero, who reigned in the AD 60s, then this would constitute powerful evidence that Revelation was written in the AD 60s.

Preterists begin their count of Roman emperors with Julius Caesar, and voilà, the sixth ends up being Nero, who ruled during the AD 60s.[20] This "proves" the book of Revelation has an early date—in the AD 60s. There is another phrase that might be helpful to commit to memory: Just as DOMITIAN = LATE DATE, so NERO = EARLY DATE. If Revelation was written during Nero's reign, as preterists try to argue, then the book of Revelation would have an early date.

This emperor-counting method of dating Revelation is not trustworthy. There are a variety of schemes for counting the seven emperors or kings in Revelation 17:10. Many questions are raised: With which emperor should one begin counting? Should all the emperors be counted, or only those deified by an act of the Roman senate? Should the brief reigns of lesser emperors be counted? The way preterists engage in the count is all too convenient to their theology. Indeed, "in order for Nero to be the sixth king, certain kings are not counted (ones with short reigns) and the starting point must be adjusted to arrive at Nero."[21] Preterists begin counting with Julius Caesar, but one could just as easily begin counting with Caesar Augustus or even Caligula. But then one wouldn't end up with Nero as the sixth. *Preterist theology obviously guides their selection of the king with which they begin their count!* Preterists are on very thin ice in choosing to use such an untrustworthy method in determining the date of Revelation.

I wrote a book titled *40 Days Through Revelation*. In it, I demonstrated that the "seven heads" in Revelation 17:10 are not seven successive Roman emperors, but rather, are seven rulers over seven different kingdoms—five of which have fallen, one still exists, and one is yet to come. At the time of John's writing, the Egyptian, Assyrian, Babylonian, Medo-Persian, and Greek empires had fallen. Rome still existed in John's day. The antichrist's kingdom was yet to come. So, Revelation 17:10 does not refer to seven Roman emperors anyway. This being so, there is no support here for an early date of Revelation.

• • •

Some preterists say supportive evidence for the book of Revelation being written during the reign of Nero relates to the number of the beast, 666. Preterists reason that because the Gematria value of Nero is 666, Revelation 13 (which speaks of the beast, or the antichrist) must refer to Nero. (The term *Gematria* refers to the practice of assigning a number to a name.) In this theory, Revelation 13 allegedly prophesies various events in Nero's life in the AD 60s, leading up to Rome's destruction of Jerusalem and the Jewish temple in AD 70. The persecutions of Nero are viewed as the great tribulation.

The preterist claim that the number 666 fits the Gematria value of Nero is not convincing. The titles of other first-century Roman rulers also yield the number 666. Nero is therefore not unique.

Aside from this, for the number 666 to fit the Gematria value of Nero, his name *and* title, "Nero Caesar," must be used. Nero had many names and titles. So, why choose "Nero Caesar"? The answer is simple. Preterists want the biblical data to support a reference to Nero, who was in power in the AD 60s and therefore fits the preterist scenario of an AD 70 destruction of Jerusalem and the temple under Nero.[22] *Choosing this name and title seems all too convenient for the preterist view.*

A literal reading of Revelation 13:17 would seem to disallow the use of titles and require only a name. Our text refers to "the number of its name"—that is, the number of the beast's name. It does not say "the number of its name *and its title*."

We can observe that the early church fathers do not corroborate the identification of Nero with the number 666. This is significant because preterists claim it is *obvious* that the number points to Nero. Those closest to the time of John's writing do not support the preterist understanding. Furthermore, it is highly revealing that the first mention of "Nero Caesar" in connection with the number 666 did not come until the nineteenth century. If the connection between Nero Caesar and 666 is so obvious, why did it take almost 1,800 years for someone to see it?[23]

Against the preterist view is the fact that if Nero were indeed the first beast of Revelation 13, then we'd expect to see him doing the things Scripture prophesies he would do. But this is not the case. Revelation 13 informs us that this individual will rule the world for 42 months, that all people on earth will worship him, that he will be killed and then be resurrected, that a second beast will support him and do great miracles (including bringing fire from heaven), that an image of the beast will be animated and speak and be placed in the Jewish temple, that all who do not worship this image will be executed, and that everyone on earth must take the mark of the beast if they want to engage in any form of commerce. Preterists should be challenged to explain when these prophecies were fulfilled during the reign of Nero.

Another problem preterists have no answers for is this: If Nero is the first beast of Revelation 13:1-10, *then who is the second beast* (13:11-18)? No individual lived during the time of Nero that fits the description of the second beast.[24] Because this second beast plays a crucial role in exalting the first beast before the entire world, he is obviously a prominent personality. And yet, in preterist theology, he apparently does not exist. Preterists should be pressed to explain this.

• • •

The preponderance of evidence supports a late date for the book of Revelation. This renders preterism unfeasible. In the next chapter, we will continue our examination of preterism with a focus on the "soon" fulfillment of Bible prophecies.

EXAMINING THE PRETERIST CASE FOR THE "SOON" FULFILLMENT OF PROPHECY

Words can have different nuances of meaning. The word *trunk*, for example, can refer to the front of an elephant, the back of a car, the bottom of a tree, or the rear end of a person. Context is always determinative in correctly understanding the term.

The same is true of the words that are written in the Bible. Depending on the context, biblical words can carry different nuances of meaning—especially in New Testament Greek, which is a particularly rich language. Examples include "soon" (Greek: *tachos*) and "near" (Greek: *eggus*) as related to the fulfillment of Bible prophecy. Let's consider the details.

* * *

Some verses in Revelation indicate a "soon" fulfillment of prophecy (Revelation 1:1, 3; 22:6, 7, 10, 12, 20). Preterists claim Revelation was written in the mid-60s AD. Therefore, this "soon" fulfillment must refer to AD 70, when Jesus "came" in judgment against Jerusalem through the Roman army.

Hank Hanegraaff says that "John's repeated use of such words and phrases as *soon* and *the time is near* demonstrate conclusively that John could not have had the twenty-first century in mind."[1] Hanegraaff says that "unlike the *Left Behind* authors, we believe that when John in Revelation says ten or more times that the events about which he is writing 'must soon take place,' or for which 'the time is near,' that is precisely what he means."[2] Kenneth Gentry likewise comments: "John clearly expects the soon fulfillment of his prophecy."[3] Gary DeMar refers to words like "soon" and "near" as *time texts* that demand the fulfillment of Revelation during the first century.[4]

At first glance, this seems like a convincing argument. But I again remind you of what Solomon said, "The one who states his case first seems right, until the other comes and examines him" (Proverbs 18:17). As related to the preterist debate, we might adapt Solomon's advice this way: "The preterist view of the 'soon' and 'near' fulfillment of prophecy might seem right until the other comes and examines him." I will examine the preterist view of "soon" and "near" throughout the rest of this chapter. There are five initial points I wish to make:

1. Foremost, church history is no friend of preterists regarding their view of the "soon" and "near" fulfillment of prophecy. The Didache, for example, is an ancient manual of Christianity that dates to the end of the first century and the beginning of the second. This document—which slightly postdates the events of AD 70—holds that Christ's prophetic Olivet Discourse points to the end times, not to a "soon" destruction of Jerusalem.

Likewise, Justin Martyr—an early second-century Christian apologist and philosopher—disagrees with the preterist view:

Two advents of Christ have been announced: the one, in which He is set forth as suffering, inglorious, dishonored, and crucified; but the other, in which He shall come from heaven with glory, when the man of apostasy, who speaks strange things against the Most High, shall venture to do unlawful deeds on the earth against us the Christians... The rest of the prophecy shall be fulfilled at His Second Coming.[5]

Justin Martyr wrote these words more than 50 years *after* the destruction of Jerusalem in AD 70. This shows that, despite his awareness of the events in AD 70, he did not believe they were a fulfillment of the book of Revelation.

It is telling that there are no first- or second-century preterists that lend support to the "soon" viewpoint of preterists. Futurist Thomas Ice has debated preterist Kenneth Gentry, and tells us that "Dr. Gentry is unable to produce any first-century or early second-century preterists from church history. In fact, Dr. Gentry admits that systematic preterism can only be traced to 1614."[6]

2. If the preterist view is wrong, as futurists believe it is, then how is the word "soon" to be interpreted? There are several interpretive options. Some believe the word "soon" should be interpreted in view of the timelessness and eternality of God. Oecumenius authored a Greek commentary on the book of Revelation that dates to the sixth century AD. He noted that even though he was writing more than 500 years after the time of Christ, the "soon" events in the book of Revelation had still not transpired:

Why does he [John] wish to add "what must soon take place," although those events which will take place have not yet occurred, even though a considerable span of time has passed, more than five hundred years, since these words were spoken? Because to the eyes of the eternal and endless God, all ages are regarded as nothing, for, as the prophet says, "A thousand years in your sight, O Lord, are as yesterday when it is past, or as a watch in the night."[7]

3. Others offer a similar viewpoint, suggesting that "soon" is a relative term. A person standing at the microwave oven who says, "Soon, I will be eating a big bowl of popcorn" indicates that "soon," in their case, is just a few minutes away. A woman in the third month of her pregnancy who says, "I will soon give birth" indicates that "soon" will involve another six months. For a husband whose wife dies, he might speak these affectionate words at her funeral: "My dear, I will be with you soon enough in heaven." In this case, "soon" refers to the remainder of his natural lifetime, which could be decades. Because "soon" is a relative term, references to the word in the book of Revelation need not refer to events in the first century. When one considers the timelessness and eternality of God, "soon" could easily refer to an extended time.

4. Some believe that the book of Revelation speaks of a long train of events, and the word "soon" refers only to the beginning of the train of events. This long train of events spans many centuries, perhaps even millennia. The train begins with a description of Jesus in glory in Revelation 1. This is followed by His interaction among the seven churches of Asia Minor of John's day (2–3). The train then runs through history, and into the future, up till the eternal state described in chapters 21–22. Nineteenth century Bible commentator Albert Barnes writes:

> It is not necessary to suppose that the meaning is that all that there is in the book [of Revelation] was soon to happen. It may mean that the series of events which were to follow on in their proper order was soon to commence... The first in the series of events was soon to begin, and the others would follow on in their train, though a portion of

them, in the regular order, might be in a remote futurity. If we suppose that there was such an order—that a series of transactions was about to commence, involving a long train of momentous developments, and that the beginning of this was to occur soon—the language used by John would be what would be naturally employed to express it…It is customary to speak of a succession of events or periods as near, however vast or interminable the series may be, when the commencement is at hand.[8]

5. Perhaps the best solution involves a proper linguistic understanding of the term "soon." The Greek word for "soon" in Revelation 1:1 ("the things that must *soon* take place") is *tachos*. The word can mean "soon" or "shortly," as preterists believe. However, Greek scholars note there are other relevant nuances of meaning.

- William F. Arndt and F. Wilbur Gingrich, in their definitive *Greek-English Lexicon of the New Testament*, say the word can mean "quick," "swift," or "speedy."[9] It can refer to that which happens quickly or speedily.

- In his *Greek-English Lexicon of the New Testament*, Joseph Thayer agrees, noting that the word can mean "quickly" or "speedily."[10]

- *The Expository Dictionary of New Testament Words*, by W.E. Vine, agrees that it can mean "swift," "quick," or "quickly."[11]

Given this, the word need not mean that the events in Revelation would occur soon from John's vantage point (in the first century) but can simply mean that when the events first begin to transpire, they will unfold *quickly, speedily*, and *swiftly*. Hence, these words in Revelation refer not to *soon events* but to *swiftly unfolding events*. As well-respected Bible commentator G.H. Lange puts it, the Greek word (*tachos*) here "does not mean *soon* but *swiftly*. It shows *rapidity of action*."[12]

I find it significant that the most common meaning of *tachos* is "swiftness of motion," not "soon." For example, the word *tachos* is used in reference to walking *fast*, talking *fast*, burning *quickly*, working *quickly*, and rowing *fast*. There are many other such examples.[13]

Today's most respected Greek grammar is *A Greek Grammar of the New Testament and Other Early Christian Literature*, edited by F. Blass, A. Debrunner, and Robert W. Funk. It categorizes adverbs into four categories:

1. Adverbs of manner.

2. Adverbs of place.

3. Adverbs of time.

4. And correlative adverbs.[14]

This definitive *Greek Grammar* categorizes the *tachos* family as *all* being "adverbs of manner." No example from the *tachos* family is listed under "adverbs of time." As related to the book of Revelation, *tachos* is not descriptive of *when* the events will occur and our Lord will come, but rather of the *manner* in which they will take place when they occur. The word indicates that when the prophecies start to be fulfilled, they will unfold "with swiftness," "quickly," or "at a rapid pace."[15]

How does this linguistic insight relate to Revelation 1:1: "The revelation of Jesus Christ, which God gave him to show to his servants the things that must *soon take place*" (emphasis added)? It simply means that the prophetic revelation in the book speaks of seven years of events in the tribulation period that will *take place speedily* or "in swift succession." For the duration of this seven-year period, one prophetic event will occur rapidly after the previous event in swift succession.[16] To be more specific, the seal judgments will unfold quickly, followed by the trumpet judgments that will speedily be unleashed, followed by the bowl judgments that will fall upon the earth in swift succession. *It will all happen quickly!*

• • •

Preterists also argue that the use of the term "near" (Greek: *eggus*) in Revelation 1:3 points to an AD 70 fulfillment of the prophecies in Revelation. However, this term need not point to a first-century fulfillment of prophecy. My late friend and colleague Norman Geisler explains it this way:

> The word "near" (Revelation 1:3) is the Greek word *eggus,* which means "near" or "at hand." But this is a relative term like "short" and "long," of which one can ask *how near?* And as measured *by whom?* What is long for us is short for God. Peter said, "With the Lord a day is like a thousand years, and a thousand years are like a day" (2 Peter 3:8 [NIV]). Further, there are clear biblical examples where a "short" time was really a long time for us. Hebrews 10:37 says Jesus would come in just "a little while," and it has been nearly 2,000 years since then, and He has not come yet.[17]

Another possibility is that the term "near" may be intended to communicate the imminence of Christ's coming. Mark Hitchcock suggests, "These events are *near* in that they are the next events on God's prophetic calendar. There is a nearness or 'at-hand-ness' of the time...The imminent return of Jesus and the need to be ready are expressed by Jesus repeatedly in the Olivet Discourse (Matt. 24:36, 42, 44; 25:10–13)."[18] The fact that the coming is *near* may thus indicate that Christ's coming could happen *at any moment* (see 1 Corinthians

4:5; 15:51-52; 16:22; Philippians 3:20; 4:5; 1 Thessalonians 1:10; James 5:7-9; 1 John 2:28).

Notice that Revelation 1:3 speaks of the connection between imminence and obedience: "Blessed are those who hear, and who keep what is written in it, for the time is near." *The Moody Bible Commentary* explains: "*For the time is near* (v. 3) gives the motivation for living in obedience: Christ may return at any time and when He does, He will hold men accountable for the lives that they have lived."[19]

There is a final point worthy of consideration. Preterists who claim that "near" and "soon" prove beyond doubt that the fulfillment of these verses must come in the first century inadvertently find themselves in an interpretive quandary. The problem surfaces in Revelation 1:1: "The revelation of Jesus Christ, which God gave him to show to his servants the things that must soon take place." The use of the word "soon" in this verse applies to *the whole book of Revelation*—including the sections on the second coming of Christ (Revelation 19:11-21) as well as the judgment of humankind and the eternal state of heaven and hell that follows (21–22).[20] In other words, these events are a part of "the revelation of Jesus Christ, which God gave him to show to his servants the things that must soon take place." As Hitchcock puts it, "These timing statements are strategically located to frame the entire content of Revelation...The preterist interpretation of these timing terms requires fulfillment in AD 70 of *the entire Apocalypse*."[21]

It will simply not do to claim that "soon" refers only to the tribulation period (Revelation 4–18) and then exempt the eternal state (chapters 19–22) from also happening "soon." The term "soon" refers to the *entire book of Revelation*. This is an inconvenient truth for preterists.

Theologian Wayne Grudem, author of the best-selling textbook *Systematic Theology: An Introduction to Biblical Doctrine*, concludes that preterists are reminiscent of Hymenaeus and Philetus. In 2 Timothy 2:17-18, we read of "Hymenaeus and Philetus, who have swerved from the truth, saying that the resurrection has already happened."

Grudem says this "is similar to the preterist claim that all the end-times events have already occurred."[22]

∙ ∙ ∙

In His Olivet Discourse, Jesus declared, "This generation will not pass away until all these things take place" (Matthew 24:34). Preterists believe that "all these things"—all the things predicted in Matthew 24:15-31—were fulfilled in AD 70 in the "generation" that heard these words of Jesus. Gentry declares that Jesus "urges his hearers, as John does his own, to expect these judgments in their own lifetimes."[23] Indeed, "this statement of Christ is indisputably clear—and absolutely demanding of a first-century fulfillment of the events in the preceding verses, including the Great Tribulation."[24] R.C. Sproul concurs: "I am convinced that the substance of the Olivet Discourse was fulfilled in A.D. 70."[25] DeMar agrees: "An honest assessment of Scripture can lead to no other conclusion."[26]

Contrary to this viewpoint, many evangelicals believe Christ was simply saying that those people who witness the signs stated earlier in Matthew 24—such as the abomination of desolation (verse 15) and "the great tribulation" (verse 21)—will see the coming of Jesus Christ within *that* very generation. Since it was common knowledge among the Jews that the future tribulation period would last only seven years (Daniel 9:24-27), it is evident that those living at the beginning of this time would likely live to see the second coming seven years later (except for those who lose their lives during this tumultuous time).

Why does "this generation" in Matthew 24:34 not refer to Christ's contemporaries? Because that generation did not witness "all these things" of which Jesus so clearly spoke. Only the generation that witnesses *those specific prophetic things* will not pass away until all the events of the tribulation period are literally fulfilled.

New Testament scholar Darrell Bock, a longtime professor at Dallas Theological Seminary, explains:

What Jesus is saying is that the generation that sees the
beginning of the end, also sees its end. When the signs come,
they will proceed quickly; they will not drag on for many
generations. It will happen within a generation...Jesus says
that when the signs of the beginning of the end come, then
the end will come relatively quickly, within a generation.[27]

Significantly, Christ's words about "this generation" (Matthew
24:34) are in the same context as His parable of the fig tree (verse
32). As explained by Thomas Ice:

When the fig tree starts to bud, you can virtually count
the days until summer. Likewise, from the time when the
actual birth-pang signs begin, there is a set time until all
these things will be fulfilled—seven years, to be exact. The
Olivet Discourse covers a relatively short period of time,
not a long eschatological age...The generation that sees
the start of it will be the same one that sees the fulfillment
of all the things Christ predicted.[28]

In view of such facts, Matthew 24:34 does not pack the punch
against pretribulationism that preterists hope for.

• • •

Preterists note that Jesus said some of His followers standing
nearby would not taste death until they saw Him coming in His
kingdom (Luke 9:27; see also Matthew 16:28). They say that given
Jesus' words, prophecies of the second coming must have been fulfilled during that generation—apparently in AD 70, when Rome
overran Jerusalem. Gentry says that the coming of the kingdom of
God with power, referenced in Mark 9:1, "almost certainly refers to
the destruction of the temple at the behest of Christ."[29]

Contrary to this view, many evangelicals believe Jesus' reference to coming in His kingdom alludes to His transfiguration, which happened precisely one week later (Matthew 17:1-13). In this view, the transfiguration served as a preview of the kingdom, in which the divine Messiah would appear in glory. This was the majority view of the early church fathers.

I find it relevant that all three Synoptic gospels follow Christ's prediction of "coming in his kingdom" with the account of the transfiguration. Moreover, Bible scholar Richard Mayhue points to the "unfortunate chapter division between Matthew 16:28 and 17:1." (Chapter divisions and verse numbers in the text of Scripture are man-made. They are not in the original manuscripts.) Because there is a chapter division between these verses, some might be led to believe there is no connection between Christ's prophecy in Matthew 16:28 of "coming in his kingdom" and the transfiguration in Matthew 17. A look at Mark 9 and Luke 9, parallel references, clears everything up, for there is no intervening chapter break in these two Gospels. This lends strong contextual support to the idea that the transfiguration is indeed a fulfillment of the prophecy.[30]

Notice that in Matthew 16:28, Jesus says, "*some* standing here" will witness the Son of Man coming in His kingdom. Matthew 17:1 then tells us that "after six days Jesus took with him Peter and James, and John" and "led them up a high mountain by themselves." So, the mention of "some" in Matthew 16:28 refers to "Peter and James, and John" (Matthew 17:1). These three saw a manifestation of Christ's kingdom power and glory. We conclude that Matthew 16:28 refers to a prophetic preview of Christ's future second-coming glory on the Mount of Transfiguration. From a contextual standpoint, this view makes great sense.

* * *

References to a "soon" and "near" fulfillment of prophecy in the book of Revelation do not necessitate a first-century fulfillment. Rather, these words are perfectly compatible with pretribulationism. In the next chapter, we will consider further preterist arguments regarding God's judgment of Jerusalem in AD 70.

7

EXAMINING THE PRETERIST CASE FOR AN AD 70 FULFILLMENT OF PROPHECY

R eimagining" titles have gained significant momentum in the Christian publishing industry in recent years. Christian books include *Reimagining Church*, *Reimagining Jesus*, *Reimagining Evangelism*, and *Reimagining the Way You Relate to God*. Secular books include *Reimagining Shakespeare*, *Reimagining Capitalism*, *Reimagining Workplace Well-being*, and *Reimagining the Humanities*.

Many people are unaware of just how drastic the reimagining can be. To illustrate, please allow me to tell you a humorous story. I promise—we'll get serious again right after the story.

Imagine for a moment that I am a New Age health guru (*I know, it's hard to imagine*). Also imagine that I'm being interviewed on television. The TV host says to me, "I know I need to stay away from fried chicken, right?" I immediately respond, "There is no need to avoid fried chicken. Just think about it. What is the chicken fried in? It's fried in vegetable oil. So, every time you eat fried chicken, you're ingesting plenty of vegetables into your body from that healthy vegetable oil. So, eat as much fried chicken as you wish."

The TV host, with a surprised look on her face, then asks me about red meat. "Red meat is great for you," I tell her. "Just think about it for a moment. What is it that cows eat every single day? *Grass!* Cows eat grass, grass, and more grass. That means that every time you eat red meat, you are ingesting plenty of healthy greens into your body, so eat as much red meat as you desire."

With a look of amazement (perhaps shock!) on her face, the TV host asks a final question: "What is your opinion about aerobic exercise?" I respond, "I strongly recommend against aerobic exercise. Our most recent research indicates that each one of us has a predetermined number of heartbeats, and we cannot exceed that number. Why would you want to use up a lot of those heartbeats really quickly by doing aerobic exercise? If you want to live longer, be a couch potato."

Okay, end of story. The word *reimagine* means to "conceive something in a whole new way." I think you can see that I—as a pretend New Age health guru—have reimagined the dangers and benefits of fried chicken, red meat, and aerobic exercise. Of course, my reimaginations could hardly be further from the truth—so don't take to heart the recommendations of this particular guru!

Preterists have reimagined key terms related to Bible prophecy. In their scenario, Babylon is sinful Jerusalem in the first century. The tribulation period refers to the AD 66–70 Jewish-Roman war. The judgments in the book of Revelation refer to God's judgment and destruction of Jerusalem. Roman emperor Nero is the antichrist. Christ's second coming is a coming "in the clouds" in judgment on the Jews. I believe these theological reimaginings are way off the mark. Please allow me to explain why.

* * *

Preterists typically teach that Babylon (the "prostitute") in the book of Revelation refers to first-century sinful Jerusalem, worthy of destruction in AD 70. Because of Israel's covenant unfaithfulness, the nation was often described as a prostitute in Old Testament times (Isaiah 1:21; Jeremiah 2:20-24, 30-33; 3:1-3, 8; Ezekiel 16; 23; Hosea 9:1). Moreover, Jerusalem was responsible for killing Old Testament prophets and New Testament apostles and saints (Matthew 23:35; Luke 11:50-51; Acts 7:52).

Jerusalem ("Babylon") was accordingly destroyed by God using the whipping rod of the Roman Empire in the first century. God's punishment of Jerusalem was unleashed when Rome overran Jerusalem and the Jewish temple in AD 70.[1]

In support of this view, preterists point to Revelation 11:8 and 16:19, where Jerusalem is called "the great city." Jerusalem must be Babylon, they say, because Babylon is also called "the great city" in Revelation 17:18. This point seems like a good argument for preterism at first glance. But as I often do, I urge you to keep Solomon's words in mind: "The one who states his case first seems right, until the other comes and examines him" (Proverbs 18:17).

Foundationally, the single best evidence against preterism is that the book of Revelation was written not before AD 70, as preterists claim, but in the mid-90s. (Please review chapter 5: "Examining the Preterist Case for an Early Date of Revelation.") That being the case, Revelation must refer to events that are *yet future* from the vantage point of AD 90. The prophecies in Revelation therefore do not point to an AD 70 destruction of Jerusalem (wrongly labeled as "Babylon").

There are also details about "the prostitute"—or "Babylon" as a false religion—that simply do not fit Jerusalem. For example, in Revelation 17:1, the great prostitute is said to "rule over many waters," meaning that it exercises control over many nations around the world. The idea that Jerusalem ever ruled over many countries around the world is absurd. To the contrary, during the extended "times of the

Gentiles" of which Jesus spoke (Luke 21:24), Gentile powers have ruled over—*and will continue to rule over*—Jerusalem until the second coming of Christ. (This extended period of Gentile dominion over Jerusalem began with the Babylonian captivity in 605 BC.)

Moreover, Revelation 17:15 tells us that the "prostitute" (religious Babylon) exercised influence over the world's general population—over the "peoples and multitudes and nations and languages." When and how did Jerusalem exercise influence over all the people of the world in or around AD 70?

Still further, Revelation 17:3 tells us that the "prostitute" controlled the antichrist and his forces for a time. Preterists interpret the antichrist as being the mighty Roman emperor, Nero. How could Jerusalem possibly control Emperor Nero and his powerful military forces? Such an idea is simply not credible.

One of the biggest problems with the Babylon = Jerusalem scenario relates to Revelation 18:21-23. This passage informs us that Babylon was to be so utterly destroyed that it will *never rise again*—just like Sodom and Gomorrah. If AD 70 represents the fulfillment of this passage, with the destruction of Jerusalem, then Revelation 18:21-23 demands that Jerusalem can *never be rebuilt again*. Therein lies the difficulty: *Jerusalem has already been rebuilt.* Israel became a nation again in 1948, and the city of Jerusalem still stands today! Not only that, but from a premillennial perspective, Jerusalem will rise to great prominence during Christ's future millennial kingdom (see Isaiah 2:3; Zechariah 14:16; Revelation 20:9).

What about the claim that Jerusalem must be Babylon since both are called "the great city" (Jerusalem in Revelation 11:8, and Babylon in 16:19 and 17:18)? This is a case of mistaken identity. Logicians might call it a "false equivalence." Those well-versed in hermeneutics call it an "illegitimate totality transfer." That phrase might seem a little confusing, so pastor Andy Woods helps us to understand it: "The argument that 'the great city' of Revelation 17–18 is identical to 'the great city' of Jerusalem found earlier in Revelation 11:8 represents a hermeneutical error known as 'illegitimate totality transfer.' This error arises when the meaning of a word or phrase as derived from its use elsewhere is then automatically read into the same word or phrase in a foreign context."[2] Context is *always* determinative in seeking to understand the various nuances of meaning in New Testament words and phrases.

We might illustrate an "illegitimate totality transfer" by noting that in the New International Version (NIV), Lucifer is called "morning star" in Isaiah 14:12, whereas Jesus is called the "Morning Star" in Revelation 22:16. Are we to conclude that Jesus is Lucifer? *By no means!* We are dealing with two entirely different contexts. In Isaiah 14:12, Lucifer is called "morning star" apparently in reference to his luminescent qualities, having been originally created by God as a glorious angel. Jesus is called "Morning Star" in Revelation 22:16 as a symbol of the divine Messiah. Just as we must not confuse the references to the "morning star," so we must not confuse the references to the "great city." Here, we recall the exhortation in Scripture to be careful in "rightly dividing the word of truth" (2 Timothy 2:15 KJV).

There are still further arguments against the Babylon = Jerusalem view. For example:

1. Jerusalem is not a city of unfathomable wealth, as is New Babylon (Revelation 18).

2. One wonders what creative interpretation preterists would assign to Revelation 18:3 when speaking of Babylon: "The merchants of the earth have grown rich from the power of her luxurious living." We must ask: When did the merchants of the earth grow rich from any so-called "luxurious living" in Jerusalem?

3. Revelation 18:9, 15 speaks of how merchants worldwide weep and wail at Babylon's destruction. One must ask:

When did the merchants of the world weep and wail when Jerusalem ("Babylon") was destroyed in AD 70?

4. There is not a single example in Jewish literature of the use of the term *Babylon* to mean Jerusalem.

5. Not a single church father taught this view.

6. There is no reference to the Jerusalem = Babylon theory in more than 2,000 years of theological writings.

Contrary to the preterist view, there is good reason to take references to Babylon in Revelation 17–18 as a literal city along the Euphrates River, and not Jerusalem. I say this because:

- Other geographical locations in the book of Revelation are intended to be taken literally, such as the seven churches in seven cities in Asia Minor (Revelation 2–3). Babylon should likewise be taken as a literal city.

- Other references to Babylon throughout the rest of the Bible always point to the literal city of Babylon. Why make an exception in the book of Revelation?

- A key geographical marker is mentioned in Revelation in association with Babylon—the Euphrates River (Revelation 16:12). This shows Babylon should be understood as the literal city of Babylon.

- Revelation 17–18 draws heavily from Jeremiah 50–51 and Isaiah 13:19-22. Both of these Old Testament passages speak of the prophetic future of the literal city of Babylon. That being so, Revelation 17–18 should also be taken as referring to the literal city of Babylon, which sits alongside the Euphrates River.

* * *

Preterists argue that references to three-and-a-half years in the book of Revelation do not refer to half of the tribulation period, but to one of the worst periods of tribulation in Jewish history—the AD 66–70 Jewish-Roman war that culminated in the destruction of Jerusalem and its temple. In Revelation 11:1-2, we read the words of John:

> I was given a measuring rod like a staff, and I was told, "Rise and measure the temple of God and the altar and those who worship there, but do not measure the court outside the temple; leave that out, for it is given over to the nations, and they will trample the holy city for forty-two months."

Preterists say these 42 months refer to the time period when Rome invaded and overcame Jerusalem. This allegedly took place from "early spring, A.D. 67 to early September, A.D. 70."[3] We are told: "The fact is that it took almost exactly forty-two months for Rome to get into a position to destroy the Temple in the Jewish War of A.D. 67–70."[4]

From a historical perspective, a significant problem with this view is that the Jewish war began in AD 66, not in the early spring of AD 67. Why omit all of AD 66? Mark Hitchcock is correct in saying that "since the war began in A.D. 66, one cannot arbitrarily move the date forward one year to achieve a predetermined outcome."[5] This historical difficulty deals a hard blow to the preterist position.

Preterists also cite Revelation 9:1-5 to support their view:

> The fifth angel blew his trumpet, and I saw a star fallen from heaven to earth, and he was given the key to the shaft of the bottomless pit. He opened the shaft of the bottomless pit, and from the shaft rose smoke like the smoke of a great furnace, and the sun and the air were

darkened with the smoke from the shaft. Then from the smoke came locusts on the earth, and they were given power like the power of scorpions of the earth. They were told not to harm the grass of the earth or any green plant or any tree, but only those people who do not have the seal of God on their foreheads. They were allowed to torment them for five months, but not to kill them, and their torment was like the torment of a scorpion when it stings someone.

Preterists claim that verse 5—"They were allowed to torment them for five months"—describes the five months from April through August AD 70, when General Titus laid siege to Jerusalem.[6] They suggest that the locust-like creatures are not the Roman army but are demons who afflicted and possessed the Jewish people during the final siege of Jerusalem.[7]

A serious problem with this interpretation is that the days do not add up. The five-month period preterists cite—April through August AD 70—totals 134 days. In Revelation, however, John uses a thirty-day-per-month calendar. This means that five months would total up to 150 days. The preterist scenario is off by sixteen days.[8]

Further, there is no external evidence—for example, from Jewish historian Flavius Josephus—that a massive horde of demons was released from the abyss during the Roman siege of Jerusalem.[9] Because Josephus documented so much of what historically took place among the Jews, one wonders what might explain such a significant omission. Surely it would have been observable and worthy of documentation. A viable explanation for Josephus's "omission" is that *it simply did not occur.*

Preterists admit to this problem. But they suggest that the barbaric conduct of the Jews during the siege provides ample evidence of demonic affliction. However, could it be that a better explanation for the so-called Jewish "barbarism" is that the Jews were being viciously attacked and were seeking to mount a defense in the face of an over-whelmingly powerful (and vicious) enemy—the Roman army? The preterist interpretation seems forced.

Another example of a forced approach relates to Revelation 14:19-20, where we read of bridle-deep carnage. Preterists claim this passage corresponds to Josephus's description of the carnage in the Jewish revolt. However, a comparison of Revelation 14:19-20 and Josephus undermines this claim.[10] There are too many dissimilarities between the two accounts. Preterists appear to be overreaching.

Preterist interpretations are obviously motivated by the desire to find correspondences between the judgments of Revelation and the events of the Jewish War. To accomplish this, they often engage in highly imaginative hermeneutics. For example, Revelation 16:18-19 tells us, "There were flashes of lightning, rumblings, peals of thunder, and a great earthquake such as there had never been since man was on the earth, so great was that earthquake. The great city was split into three parts." The problem for preterists is that no earthquakes occurred during the Jewish revolt. Resorting to allegory, they inter-pret the devastating, world-record earthquake as the division of Jeru-salem "into three bickering factions" during Rome's conquest of the city.[11] I do not believe this is a credible interpretation.

* * *

Some preterists (*full* preterists) claim that Christ's second coming involved a coming of Christ in judgment against the Jews. It was a "cloud coming"—a coming of Christ *in the clouds*. Preterists appeal to Revelation 1:7, which speaks of the second coming: "Behold, he is coming with the clouds, and every eye will see him, even those who pierced him, and all tribes of the earth will wail on account of him." Kenneth Gentry appeals to the Old Testament to add sup-port to his view:

> In the Old Testament, clouds are frequently employed
> as symbols of divine wrath and judgment. Often God is
> seen surrounded with foreboding clouds which express
> His unapproachable holiness and righteousness. Thus,
> God is poetically portrayed in certain judgment scenes
> as coming in the clouds to wreak historical vengeance
> upon His enemies.[12]

Gentry cites the following verses as examples of this phenomena: 2 Samuel 22:8, 10; Psalms 18:7-15; 68:4, 33; 97:2-9; 104:3; Isaiah 13:9; 19:1; 26:21; 30:27; Joel 2:1-2; Micah 1:3; Nahum 1:2ff; Zephaniah 1:14-15. He then relates these verses about *God* in the clouds to Revelation 1:7, where *Christ* is in the clouds: "The New Testament picks up this apocalyptic judgment imagery when it speaks of Christ's coming in clouds of judgment during history."[13]

Theologian Wayne Grudem rebuts: "The claim of preterists that Christ's second coming occurred when he returned invisibly in judgment in the destruction of the Jerusalem temple in AD 70 denies the evident meaning of numerous New Testament verses that predict events that clearly did not take place in AD 70 and have not yet taken place."[14]

For example, Grudem says, in Matthew 24:31, Jesus affirms that "he will send out his angels with a loud trumpet call, and they will gather his elect from the four winds, from one end of heaven to the other." When did this happen in AD 70?

In John 14:3, Jesus promises, "If I go and prepare a place for you, I will come again and will take you to myself, that where I am you may be also." When was this fulfilled in AD 70?

In Acts 1:11, an angel said to some of Christ's followers, "Men of Galilee, why do you stand looking into heaven? This Jesus, who was taken up from you into heaven, will come in the same way as you saw him go into heaven." When did Jesus come "in the same way as you saw him go into heaven" in AD 70?

We read, in 1 John 3:2, "Beloved, we are God's children now, and what we will be has not yet appeared; but we know that when he appears we shall be like him, because we shall see him as he is." When did this happen in AD 70?

Moreover, Gentry ignores a key point of dissimilarity between these "cloud comings" and Christ's coming in Revelation 1:7. I am referring to the fact that "every eye will see him." This denotes a personal, visible coming of Christ, not a hidden "cloud coming" in judgment through the Roman army in AD 70. If Christ's coming is in the clouds and is hence invisible to those on earth, then in what sense will "every eye" see Him? Gentry claims people will "see" Christ "with the 'eye of understanding' rather than the organ of vision."[15] Frankly, this reminds me of the Jehovah's Witnesses. The Watchtower book *Let God Be True* tells us that Christ's invisible second coming "is recognized by the eyes of one's understanding."[16]

It is noteworthy that Jesus Himself indicated that His second coming would be a clear and visible event. He did this in the context of warning about false teachers who say He has already come: "If they say to you, 'Look, he is in the wilderness,' do not go out. If they say, 'Look, he is in the inner rooms,' do not believe it. For as the lightning comes from the east and shines as far as the west, so will be the coming of the Son of Man" (Matthew 24:26-27). Lightning is startlingly visible. *So will be the second coming of Christ.*

Not unexpectedly, preterists take references to lightning allegorically. They suggest that Christ "will 'come' in judgment like a destructive lightning bolt against Jerusalem (v. 27)." However, they say this "coming as lightning" is not a "publicly visible, physical coming."[17]

In response, one must ask: Would a person not already predisposed toward preterism interpret the verse that way? What is the most natural understanding of the verse? Read it aloud: "As the lightning comes from the east and shines as far as the west, so will be the coming of the Son of Man." I've always believed that if the plain sense makes good sense, seek no other sense lest you end up in nonsense. To me, any interpretation of this verse that fails to recognize the visible nature of the second coming is nonsense.

One must also ask: If Jesus' second coming was to be an invisible event, wouldn't He have made that clear to His followers? Wouldn't He have corrected mistaken notions of His second coming when followers expressed belief in a physical second coming? Wouldn't He have said, "No, no—I'm not coming physically and visibly, as you see Me now. Rather, I will come spiritually in judgment upon Israel. You won't actually see Me." Theologians Paul Benware and Charles Ryrie write:

> When the disciples asked the Lord about His "coming" (presence), the usual meaning of the word—along with Zechariah's prophecy of the actual coming/presence of the Messiah—would certainly have affected both their understanding and their questions. It is very hard to believe that Jesus would not have corrected their thinking and would not have made the matter of His "coming" crystal clear. If He were to come in AD 70, in a non-literal return in judgment where He would not be visibly present, the Lord Jesus would have told His followers. And furthermore, Jesus underscores the unmistakable nature of His "coming" when He likens His coming to the spectacular lightning flashes going across the sky. His "coming" will be a powerful, glorious, and unique event, visible to all and which no one can mistake for something else (24:27).[18]

We must also challenge the preterist position that the clouds in Revelation 1:7 relate to judgment. Clouds are often used in Scripture in association with God's visible glory (Exodus 16:10; 40:34-35; 1 Kings 8:10-11; Matthew 17:5; 24:30; 26:64). The late theologian and president of Dallas Theological Seminary John F. Walvoord taught that just "as Christ was received by a cloud in His ascension (Acts 1:9), so He will come in the clouds of heaven (Matt. 24:30; 26:64; Mark 13:26; 14:62; Luke 21:27)."[19] Scripture reveals that just as Jesus left with a visible manifestation of the glory of God (clouds of glory were present), so Christ will return with a visual manifestation of the glory of God (clouds of glory will be present).

Bible expositor Philip Edgcumbe Hughes adds:

> The clouds intended here are not dark storm clouds which presage divine judgment…but the bright clouds of his transcendental glory. They stand for the shekinah glory of God's presence which caused the face of Moses to shine with supernatural brilliance…and they are to be identified with the "bright cloud" of Christ's divine glory witnessed by Peter, James, and John on the mount of transfiguration (Mt. 17:5), and with the cloud which received him out of the apostles' sight at his ascension.[20]

In Scripture, these clouds of glory are always visible. No wonder every eye on earth will see Christ when He comes again in glory. Matthew 24:30 says of the second coming, "Then will appear in heaven the sign of the Son of Man, and then all the tribes of the earth will mourn, and *they will see the Son of Man coming on the clouds of heaven with power and great glory*" (emphasis added).

The Greek words used of the second coming confirm the visual nature of Christ's coming. Thayer's *Greek-English Lexicon of the New Testament* says the word *parousia* is used in the New Testament of "the future, visible, return from heaven of Jesus, the Messiah."[21] Another Greek word used to describe the second coming of Christ in the New Testament is *apokalupsis*. This word carries the basic meaning of "revelation," "visible disclosure," "unveiling," and "removing the cover"

from something that is hidden. The word is used of Christ's second
coming in 1 Peter 4:13: "Rejoice insofar as you share Christ's suffer-
ings, that you may also rejoice and be glad *when his glory is revealed*"
(emphasis added).

Another word used of Christ's second coming in the New Testament is *epiphaneia*, which carries the basic meaning of "to appear."
Vine's Expository Dictionary of Biblical Words says *epiphaneia* literally
means "a shining forth." The dictionary provides several examples
from ancient literature of how the word points to a physical, visible appearance of someone.[22] The word is used several times by the
apostle Paul concerning Christ's visible second coming. Titus 2:13
refers to "waiting for our blessed hope, *the appearing* of the glory of
our great God and Savior Jesus Christ" (emphasis added). First Timothy 6:14 exhorts us to "keep the commandment unstained and free
from reproach until *the appearing* of our Lord Jesus Christ" (emphasis
added). Significantly, Christ's first coming—which was both bodily
and visible ("the Word became flesh," John 1:14)—was called an *epiphaneia* (2 Timothy 1:10). In the same way, Christ's second coming
will be both bodily and visible.

We conclude that it is the consistent testimony of Scripture—
whether the word *parousia*, *apokalupsis*, or *epiphaneia* is used—that
Christ's second coming will be visible to all humankind (see Matthew 16:27-28; 24:30; Daniel 7:13; Zechariah 9:14; 12:10; Mark 1:2;
John 1:51; 2 Timothy 4:1).

This is further confirmed in Revelation 1:7, where we are told that
at the second coming, "every eye shall see him." The Greek word for
"see" in this verse is *horao*. In the *Greek-English Lexicon of the New Testament*, William Arndt and F. Wilbur Gingrich say the word in Revelation 1:7 means "see, catch sight of, notice of sense perception."[23]
Likewise, Thayer's *Lexicon* says *horao* is used in Revelation 1:7 in the
sense, "to see with the eyes [physical organs]."[24] *Vine's Expository Dictionary of Biblical Words* defines *horao* as "bodily vision."[25] Clearly,

Revelation 1:7 refers to an observation made with the eyes—*the physical, bodily organs.*

There are still further issues that preterists have not satisfactorily answered regarding God's judgment and the destruction of Jerusalem in AD 70, and its relationship to Christ's second coming. For example:

1. Zechariah 12:3 indicates that "all the nations of the world" will come against Jerusalem. If preterism is correct, when did this occur in AD 70? Only Rome came against Jerusalem.

2. Zechariah 12:9 indicates that God will destroy all the nations that come against Jerusalem. When did this occur in AD 70? *It didn't!* This event still lies in the prophetic future.

3. The preterist view of Jesus' "cloud coming" in AD 70 fails to deal adequately with Christ's promise to "come" and deliver His people from a time of terrible persecution. Preterists do not deal with Revelation 3:10-11, where Jesus said to the church at Philadelphia: "Because you have kept my word about patient endurance, I will keep you from the hour of trial that is coming on the whole world, to try those who dwell on the earth. I am coming soon. Hold fast what you have, so that no one may seize your crown." One must ask: How did Christ's "cloud coming" in AD 70 bring deliverance for the church from a specific time of persecution? Nothing even remotely similar to this deliverance occurred in AD 70.

4. Wayne Grudem demonstrates how the Christian creeds argue against the preterist view of the second coming: "The claim that Christ has already returned contradicts some of the historic creeds of the Christian church, such as the Apostles Creed, which puts Christ's second coming

in the future when it says, 'He ascended into heaven; and sitteth at the right hand of God the Father Almighty; from thence he shall come to judge the quick and the dead.' The Nicene Creed (325/381 AD) similarly says, 'and sitteth on the right hand of the Father; and he shall come again, with glory, to judge both the quick and the dead; whose kingdom shall have no end.' The Westminster Confession of Faith says, 'and there sitteth at the right hand of his Father, making intercession, and shall return, to judge men and angels, at the end of the world' (8:4)."[26] Would preterists say that because the Apostles Creed, the Nicene Creed, and the Westminster Confession of Faith argue against preterism, the designers of these creeds were doctrinally off base?

• • •

My friend, there are just too many interpretive problems that accompany preterism. When we follow the method modeled by the Bereans and test all things against Scripture (Acts 17:11), preterism falls short in countless ways. In the next chapter, we will consider general preterist claims against pretribulationism.

EXAMINING THE PRETERIST CASE AGAINST PRETRIBULATIONISM

During the years I was on the national *Bible Answer Man* radio broadcast, we'd periodically have a preterist caller who asked in a rather challenging way, "Can you give me a single verse that explicitly teaches the doctrine of the rapture?" The implication—in both the question and the tone of the caller's voice—was that there are no such verses and that gullible pretribs have fallen for a doctrine with no biblical support.

I've also received many letters and emails through the years from Christians who heard a preterist Bible teacher—often on the radio— say the same thing. These Christians typically write to me hoping to be reassured that the rapture is a biblical doctrine.

One of the unfortunate results of prophecy under siege (and indeed, the rapture under siege) is that many well-meaning Christians are left wondering what to think. Is there a rapture, or is there not? Do pretribulationists use a faulty method in interpreting prophecy, as preterists charge? Is it true that there is no seven-year tribulation period? And what are we to make of the preterist claim that pretribs are anti-Semitic for teaching that there will be many casualties among the Jewish people during the tribulation period? Still further, are pretribs naïve for believing that a Jewish temple will be rebuilt during the tribulation period? Let's give brief consideration to these issues.

* * *

Preterists often claim that pretribulationists use a faulty method of Bible interpretation. One preterist declared that there are "dangers inherent in the interpretive method" that pretribs employ.[1] The goal of preterists is obvious. If they can undermine the interpretive method pretribs use, then they can easily undermine everything else they believe.

In truth, pretribs seek to utilize exegesis in interpreting Scripture. *Exegesis* refers to drawing the meaning out of the text of Scripture, while *eisegesis* refers to superimposing a meaning onto the text. By using eisegesis instead of exegesis, a Marxist interpreter could, for example, so skew the meaning of the US Constitution that it comes out reading like a communist document. One could make a strong case that preterists often engage in eisegesis. They so skew the meaning of the biblical text that it comes out saying something entirely different from what was intended by the author. I demonstrated in the previous chapter that preterists "reimagine" a number of issues related to Bible prophecy. Such reimagining entails extensive eisegesis.

Instead of superimposing a meaning onto the biblical text, the objective interpreter seeks to discover the author's intended meaning (the only true meaning), which cannot be altered. Meaning is *determined* by the author. It is *discovered* by readers. This is foundational to pretrib methodology.

Pretribs also believe that scripture interprets scripture. Every word in the Bible is part of a verse, and every verse is part of a paragraph, and every paragraph is part of a book, and every book is part of the whole of Scripture. No verse of Scripture can be divorced from the surrounding verses.

Interpreting Scripture thus involves an immediate context and a broader context. The immediate context of a verse is the paragraph (or paragraphs) of the biblical book in question and should always be consulted when interpreting individual verses. The broader context is the whole of Scripture. We must remember that the interpretation of a specific passage must not contradict the total teaching of Scripture on a point. Individual verses are not isolated fragments but parts of a whole. Therefore, the exposition of these verses must exhibit them in proper relation to the whole and to each other. That is why we say that scripture interprets scripture. If we would understand *the parts*, our wisest course is to get to know *the whole*. Pretribs believe that both *the parts* and *the whole* support pretribulationism.

Pretribulationists seek to be consistent in adhering to the literal (historical-grammatical) method of interpretation. Preterists, by contrast, often demonstrate a rejection of a literal method. For example, as the late apologist Norman L. Geisler notes, "Many predictions in Matthew 24–25 and Revelation 6–18 were not fulfilled in AD 70—at least not literally. For example, the stars did not fall from heaven (Mt. 24:29), nor were one-third of human beings killed (Rev. 9:18), and neither did all the creatures in the sea die (Rev. 16:3) in AD 70."[2] Preterists either ignore key verses or resort to allegory to make their preterist viewpoint fit the biblical text. Thomas Ice explains:

> Preterists...while interpreting passages that appear to fit their scheme literally (i.e., Luke 21:20-24), overall tend to allegorize key texts (i.e., Matt. 24:29-31). Allegorization occurs when an interpreter brings into a text a meaning, based upon ideas from outside the text. Thus, their interpretation cannot be supported from a normal reading of the words and phrases. A preterist example is seen when they make the word "coming" [regarding Christ's second coming] (i.e., Matt. 24:30; Rev. 1:7) to mean a non-physical,

non-bodily event. This is done, not by demonstrating that "coming" must mean that from the context, but by importing foreign concepts from other sources into a given passage. This is not a valid form of interpretation.[3]

In allegory, the text of Scripture is no longer the final authority: "The interpreter who allegorizes the text essentially becomes the final authority on the text's meaning."[4] Five different allegorical interpreters could feasibly have five entirely different interpretations of the same biblical text.

Let us take the "stars falling from heaven" as an example of preterist allegory. Instead of taking cosmic disturbances literally, Kenneth Gentry says, "Apocalyptic language is a dramatic way of expressing national calamity or victory in battle."[5] So, the destruction of Jerusalem in AD 70 was so bad it was like stars falling from heaven. Pretribulationists, by contrast, do not believe the stars falling from heaven are an allegory. There is no indication in the context that such cosmic disturbances are to be taken allegorically.

While pretribulationists reject preterist allegorical interpretations, preterists typically mischaracterize the literal method pretribs use as leaving no room for symbols and figures of speech. This is simply false. As E.R. Craven put it, "The literalist (so-called) is not one who denies that figurative language, that symbols, are used in prophecy, nor does he deny that great spiritual truth is set forth therein; his position is, simply, that the prophecies are to be normally interpreted (i.e., according to received laws of language) as any other utterances are interpreted—that which is manifestly figurative being so regarded."[6]

The pretribulationist is fully aware there are some symbols in prophetic Scripture. However, each symbol is emblematic of something literal. For example, in the book of Revelation, John said the "seven stars" in Christ's right hand were "the seven angels [or messengers] of the seven churches," and "the seven lampstands" were "the seven churches"

(Revelation 1:20). The "bowls full of incense" were "the prayers of the saints" (5:8). "The waters" were "peoples and multitudes and nations and languages" (17:15). Clearly, each symbol represents something literal.

Textual clues often point us to the literal truth found in a symbol—either in the immediate context or the broader context of the whole of Scripture. In many instances, symbols in the book of Revelation may be found in the Old Testament. One of my former professors at Dallas Theological Seminary, Dr. J. Dwight Pentecost, said that if you have six months to study the book of Revelation, you should spend the first three months studying the Old Testament because many of the symbols in Revelation are found there.

A basic rule of thumb is that when you encounter a symbol you are unsure about, consult other scriptures that relate to that symbol. For example, if you want additional information about Jesus being called a "Lamb" in Revelation 5:6, look up other verses pertaining to sacrificial lambs (for example, Exodus 12:1-13; 29:38-42; Isaiah 53:7; Jeremiah 11:19). That way, you can discover the intended literal meaning of the symbol—in this case, that Jesus was a substitutionary sacrifice for our sins.

That said, I want to reaffirm that most of the prophecies in the Bible are not symbolic but are quite literal. This is illustrated in how most Old Testament prophecies relating to the first coming of Christ were fulfilled literally (*born in Bethlehem*—Micah 5:2; *born of a virgin*—Isaiah 7:14; *pierced for our sins*—Zechariah 12:10; and so forth). In the same way, most of the prophecies dealing with the second coming—and the events leading up to the second coming—will be fulfilled just as literally. A precedent has been set. This means that if you want to understand how God will fulfill prophecy in the future, it is wise to look at how He has fulfilled prophecy in the past. We should interpret prophecies of the second coming just as literally as the prophecies of the first coming. Futurism is the natural outgrowth of a consistently literal interpretation of Scripture.

By contrast, the preterist policy seems to be: "When a literal under-standing of a biblical text does not fit my preterist theology, allego-rize it in such a way that it does fit."

* * *

Gary DeMar asks, "Can you give me one verse that explicitly teaches a pretribulational rapture?"[7] I devote an entire chapter later in this book that thoroughly establishes the biblical case for a pre-tribulational rapture (chapter 12). At this juncture, I will simply say, "Yes,"—Revelation 3:10 is among a number of verses that teach a pre-tribulational rapture: "I will keep you from the hour of trial that is coming on the whole world, to try those who dwell on the earth."

Notice the definite article (*the*) before the word *hour* in this verse ("I will keep you from *the hour* of trial"). This shows that a specific and distinctive time period is in view, not just any "hour of trial" in church history. The context points to the future seven-year tribula-tion, described in detail in Revelation 6–19. This is the hour of trial from which the church is to be kept.

Revelation 3:10 reveals that church saints will be kept from the actual *hour of testing*, not just the testing itself. If the Lord meant to communicate that He would preserve them amid the testing itself, He would have omitted the words "the hour" and simply said, "I will keep you from the testing."

The Greek preposition *ek* (translated as "from"—"I will keep you *from* the hour of trial") carries the idea of separation from something. This means that believers will be kept from the hour of testing in the sense that they will be completely separated from it by being rap-tured before the period even begins. Prophecy expert Renald Showers comments on this in his excellent book *Maranatha: Our Lord Come!*:

> The language in Jesus' reference to this future period of worldwide testing implied that it was well-known to the

church saints. It was well-known because both Old and New Testament Scriptures, written years before Revelation, foretold this unique, future period of testing or Tribulation, which would take place prior to the coming of the Messiah to rule the world in the Messianic Age or Millennium (Isa. 2:10-21; Dan. 12:1; Zeph. 1:14-18; Mt. 24:4-31).[8]

I need to clarify that Revelation 3:10 promises only that *church* saints will be kept out of this hour of trial that is coming upon the entire earth. We call them "church saints" because the promise is given in the context of Christ's words to the seven churches of Asia Minor in Revelation 2–3. In contrast to church saints, those who become believers in Christ *during* the hour of trial—those we might call "tribulation saints"—will go through the remainder of the tribulation. They will not be exempt from the hour of trial. It is crucial to recognize the distinction between church saints and tribulation saints. Messianic believer Arnold Fruchtenbaum explains:

> Throughout the Tribulation, saints are being killed on a massive scale (Rev. 6:9-11; 11:7; 12:11; 13:7, 15; 14:13; 17:6; 18:24). If these saints are Church saints, they are not being kept safe and Revelation 3:10 is meaningless. Only if Church saints and Tribulation saints are kept distinct does the promise of Revelation 3:10 make any sense.[9]

There is a theological backdrop to Fruchtenbaum's point. Some Christians are posttribulationists—they believe the rapture will occur *after* the tribulation period. They interpret Revelation 3:10 to mean that God will somehow keep believers safe through the tribulation period. Yet, the book of Revelation itself tells us that not only will the saints be severely persecuted, but many will also die as martyrs (Revelation 6:9). Revelation 13:7 informs us that the antichrist "was allowed to make war on the saints and to conquer them." Daniel 7:21 tells us the same thing: The antichrist "made war with the saints and prevailed over them." Many believers will die. The antichrist will *conquer them* and will *prevail over them.* This hardly sounds like believers will somehow be kept safe through the tribulation period.

The more sensible way to interpret these verses is that the saints who experience persecution and martyrdom during the tribulation period are specifically tribulation saints—they become believers *during* the tribulation period. This is in contrast to the church saints, who are raptured before the tribulation period even begins.

In keeping with the idea that the church will be raptured before this time of tribulation begins, no Old Testament passage on the tribulation mentions the church (Deuteronomy 4:29-30; Jeremiah 30:4-11; Daniel 8:24-27; 12:1-2). Likewise, no New Testament passage on the tribulation mentions the church (Matthew 13:30, 39-42, 48-50; 24:15-31; 1 Thessalonians 1:9-10; 5:4-9; 2 Thessalonians 2:1-11). This includes Revelation 6–18, where the tribulation period is described in detail. The church's absence from these Scripture passages indicates it is not on earth during this "hour of trial."

* * *

Some preterists claim that Christians are sustained by the hope of a future resurrection from the dead, not by a manufactured belief that they are meant to be taken away from trouble by a rapture.

This claim is easily answered from Scripture. The resurrection of dead believers is actually a part of the rapture. First Thessalonians 4:16-17 tells us: "The dead in Christ will rise first. Then we who are alive, who are left, will be caught up together with them in the clouds to meet the Lord in the air." At the rapture, dead believers are resurrected first, followed by a translation of living believers into their glorified bodies. Both groups will meet Christ in the air (1 Thessalonians 4:17).

First Corinthians 15:52-53 adds more details: "The trumpet will sound, and the dead will be raised imperishable, and we shall be changed. For this perishable body must put on the imperishable, and this mortal body must put on immortality." These verses describe the resurrection of dead believers ("the dead will be raised imperishable") and the translation of living believers into their glorified bodies ("we shall be changed"). *How glorious it will be!*

* * *

Preterists argue that verses that promise the church deliverance from God's "wrath" refer not to rescue from the wrath of the tribulation period but from God's eternal wrath reserved for the unsaved in the lake of fire. Such verses, therefore, do not support pretribulationism.

Pretribulationists are certainly thrilled that they will be delivered from God's eternal wrath that is reserved for the unsaved in the lake of fire. The salvation we have in Jesus is wondrous indeed.

That said, the "eternal-wrath view" set forth by preterists runs contrary to key prophetic Bible verses. Revelation 3:10 is an example. Recall that in Revelation 3:10, Jesus specifically promised, "I will keep you from the *hour of trial* that is coming on the whole world, to try those who dwell on the earth" (emphasis added). This "hour of trial" cannot be interpreted to mean the eternal wrath of God in the lake of fire. Rather, this verse speaks of our deliverance from a *limited period* of wrath—a period that is described in chapters 6 through 18.

Notice that Revelation 3:10 says the purpose of the hour of trial is to "try those who dwell on the earth." Bible expositor J. Dwight Pentecost points out that "those who dwell on the earth" are "earth dwellers" who are sinful and rebellious against God.[10] Aside from Revelation 3:10, these earth dwellers are referenced ten more times in the book of Revelation. "Throughout Revelation they are recognized as enemies of God, persecutors of God's people, and objects of God's wrath because of their hardened, incorrigible rebellion against the Lord."[11] Hence, we see two groups of people in Revelation 3:10—*believers* who are "kept" from the hour of trial and *earth dwellers* who are left behind to experience God's temporal judgment.

First Thessalonians 1:9-10 also refers to the deliverance of believers before God's wrath falls in the tribulation period: "You turned to God from idols to serve the living and true God, and to wait for his Son from heaven, whom he raised from the dead, Jesus who delivers us from the wrath to come." Notice the key components of verse 10: "wait for his Son from heaven...who delivers us from the wrath to come." Pretribulationists see this as an obvious reference to awaiting the imminent rapture, which will deliver us from the coming tribulation period, during which God's temporal wrath will be unleashed on the earth. This passage does not refer to God's eternal wrath in the lake of fire. Fruchtenbaum provides this insight:

> In 1 Thessalonians 1:10, the wrath of God is future and, hence, cannot refer to the general wrath of God against sin, which is a present reality. While hell and the lake of fire are also future, they cannot be what this passage is referring to. By virtue of his salvation, the believer is already redeemed from hell. Yeshua is not returning for the purpose of delivering the church from hell or the lake of fire, for this has already been done at the cross. Thus, the wrath that the church is being delivered from is the wrath of the great tribulation.[12]

We see the same in 1 Thessalonians 5:9: "God has not destined us for wrath, but to obtain salvation through our Lord Jesus Christ." The context is set for us in the preceding verses, which speak about the Day of the Lord, which begins with the tribulation period (verses 1-3). Because the context is the Day of the Lord, the "wrath" must be that which will fall during the tribulation period. Likewise, the "salvation" in this verse refers to being saved out of the tribulation period via the rapture. We might summarize 1 Thessalonians 5:9 this way: "The believer is appointed not to wrath, but to salvation; not to the Day of the Lord, but to the Rapture (pretribulationism)."[13] *The Bible Knowledge Commentary* explains:

> God's intention for them is not the wrath that will come on the earth in the day of the Lord, but the full salvation that will be theirs when the Lord returns for them in the clouds. The wrath of God referred to here clearly refers to the Tribulation; the context makes this apparent. Deliverance from that wrath is God's appointment for believers. This temporal salvation comes through the Lord Jesus Christ just as does eternal salvation.[14]

Since God's wrath in the tribulation period is so horrific, one must wonder why God would put His bride (the church) on the earth during this time. That doesn't make sense. It amounts to saying, Christ *blesses* the church by giving her eternal salvation, and then Christ *blasts* the church by putting her in the tribulation period. Christ would be saying to the church, "I've completely forgiven you of all your sins, and I love you dearly as my bride, but now you're going to suffer." *No!* Such an interpretation will not do. Our verse tells us that the church will be delivered—via the rapture—from the temporal wrath that will fall upon the world during the tribulation period.

* * *

Preterists ask, "Where in Revelation is the seven-year tribulation found?"[15]

In answering this question, I first remind you of something I said previously in this chapter: *scripture interprets scripture*. The entire Holy Scripture—both Old and New Testaments—is the context and guide for understanding the particular passages of Scripture. Individual verses are not isolated fragments, but parts of a whole. The exposition of these verses, therefore, must exhibit them in proper relation to the whole and to each other.

We can illustrate the need for scripture interpreting scripture with the doctrine of the Trinity. One might ask, "Where in the Bible is the Trinity found?" Of course, no single verse explicitly teaches the doctrine of the Trinity. But when we compare various verses about the nature of God, it becomes clear that (1) there is one, and only one, God (Deuteronomy 6:4; Isaiah 44:6; John 5:44; 1 Corinthians 8:4; 1 Timothy 2:5; James 2:19); (2) the Father is God (John 6:27; Romans 1:7; Galatians 1:1; 1 Peter 1:2); (3) Jesus is God (Titus 2:13; Hebrews 1:8; Revelation 1:17); (4) the Holy Spirit is God (Genesis 1:2; Exodus 31:3; Ezekiel 11:24; Romans 8:9, 14; 1 John 4:2); and (5) the Father, Son, and Holy Spirit are persons who are distinct from each other (Matthew 3:16-17; 2 Corinthians 13:14). Comparing all these verses, we conclude that there is one God and that within the unity of the one God are three co-equal and co-eternal persons, the Father, the Son, and the Holy Spirit.[16] Similarly, we must look at all the data derived from the book of Revelation, the book of Daniel, and other prophetic books to gain a full, composite understanding of the seven-year tribulation period. Put another way, we come to a biblical under-standing of the tribulation period as we let scripture interpret scripture.

We begin with the book of Revelation, which refers to the tribula-tion period as an "hour of trial" (Revelation 3:10). The term "hour" is not intended to communicate that the length of the tribulation period is 60 minutes, but rather that it would be a *definite time period of trial*. We must look elsewhere in Revelation (and the parallel apocalyptic book, Daniel) to find indications of a seven-year tribulation period.

Consulting Revelation reveals that the two prophetic witnesses will minister for 1,260 days, which is three-and-a-half years. This is the first half of the tribulation period (Revelation 11:3). We are also told that the antichrist will be allowed to exercise authority for 42 months (13:5), which also measures out to three-and-a-half years—the second half of the tribulation period. Interestingly, half the tribulation period is elsewhere described as "a time and times and half a time" (12:14). A "time" is one year, "times" is two years, and "half a time" is a half year—totaling three-and-a-half years. If all this is correct, we can conclude that there are two halves of the tribulation period, each lasting three-and-a-half years, which totals seven years.

As we consult the book of Daniel, we see that the tribulation period is the seventieth week of Daniel (Daniel 9:27). Just as the first 69 weeks of years involved literal years (totaling 483 years), so the seventieth week is seven literal years. This meshes quite nicely with the various references to three-and-a-half years in Revelation—each referring to either the first or the second half of the tribulation period.

• • •

Preterists charge pretribulationists with barbarism for holding to the belief that two-thirds of the Jews will die during the tribulation period. Zechariah 13:8 tells us, "In the whole land, declares the LORD, two thirds shall be cut off and perish, and one third shall be left alive." DeMar criticizes Tim LaHaye for his view on the verse: "Why isn't LaHaye warning Jews now living in Israel about this pre-determined holocaust by encouraging them to leave Israel until the conflagration is over? Instead, we find those who hold to LaHaye's position supporting relocation efforts of Jews to the land of Israel that will mean certain death for a majority of them because it's a 'fulfillment of Bible prophecy.'"[17]

Thomas Ice responds to DeMar by pointing out that "about three-fifths of the entire earth's population will be killed during the course of the seven-year tribulation, many of them believers (Rev. 6:9-11)."[18] Hence, it is unfair to accuse LaHaye of teaching a Jewish holocaust when, in fact, a holocaust will come upon the entire world—killing both Gentiles and Jews. Let's also be clear that LaHaye did not "write the letter," so to speak. He is simply the *mail carrier*. In other words, LaHaye did not write the scripture which prophesies the death of two-thirds of the Jews. Rather, he is simply delivering the message of what Scripture teaches in Zechariah 13:8.

Ice observes that one of the main purposes of the tribulation (the seventieth week of Daniel) is to bring Israel to faith in Jesus as their Messiah.[19] This necessarily requires the purging that takes place during the tribulation period. Zechariah 13:7-9 informs us that two-thirds of the Jewish people will lose their lives during the tribulation period. However, one-third—the remnant—will survive and turn to the Lord and be saved (see Isaiah 64:1-12). This represents a severe purging of unbelieving Israel, but it serves to prepare the remnant to eventually turn to the Lord for salvation at the end of the tribulation period.

Later, in the millennial kingdom, Israel—the Jewish remnant—will experience full possession of the promised land (Genesis 12:1-3; 15:18-21; 17:21; 35:10-12) and the reestablishment of the Davidic throne (2 Samuel 7:5-17). It will be a time of physical and spiritual blessing, the basis of which is the new covenant (Jeremiah 31:31-34). As Fruchtenbaum (remember, a messianic believer) puts it, the judgment of the tribulation period "will purge out the rebels among the Jewish people. Only then will the whole new nation, a regenerate nation, be allowed to enter the promised land under King Messiah."[20]

Ultimately, it really does not matter whether Jews are in Israel or any other part of the world during the tribulation period. *All* unbelievers—both Jewish and Gentile—will lose their lives in judgment before the beginning of the millennial kingdom. "At the second coming all unbelievers will be killed and prevented from going into the millennium (Matt. 13:36-43, 45-50; 25:31-46)."[21] That may not be pleasant to read. But we cannot simply excise from the pages of Scripture verses like Matthew 25:41, where Jesus says to the "goats" (unbelieving Gentiles), "Depart from me, you cursed, into the eternal fire prepared for the devil and his angels."

Ice turns the tables on DeMar by noting that many modern orthodox Jews—uninfluenced by LaHaye's books—believe that Zechariah 13:8-9 is still a future event.[22] This being the case, "why isn't DeMar warning them about the coming holocaust if he is so concerned for the welfare of modern Jewry?"[23]

As it turns out, the Jews *are* warned to get out of Jerusalem after all. The warning comes from Jesus: "When you see the abomination of desolation spoken of by the prophet Daniel, standing in the holy place (let the reader understand), then let those who are in Judea flee to the mountains. Let the one who is on the housetop not go down to take what is in his house, and let the one who is in the field not turn back to take his cloak" (Matthew 24:15-18). In other words, Jesus warns the Jews in Judea that when the antichrist defiles the local temple at the midpoint of the tribulation period, get out of town immediately. *Pronto!* We might paraphrase it, "Run for your life."

Those Jews who ignore Christ's warning will suffer persecution and even death at the hands of the antichrist. That they choose to stay behind and suffer the consequences is no one's fault but their own.

A parallel verse that speaks of God's deliverance of the Jewish remnant is Revelation 12:6: "The woman fled into the wilderness, where she has a place prepared by God, in which she is to be nourished for 1,260 days." The "woman" is the Jewish remnant. God cares for this remnant during the second half of the tribulation period.

At the end of the tribulation period, this remnant will trust in their Messiah, Jesus Christ, for salvation. Despite the loss of life of many Jews during this time, this salvation of the Jewish remnant is the ultimate good news.

• • •

Preterists claim there is no biblical support for the idea that the Jewish temple will be rebuilt. They ask, "Can you point out one verse from the New Testament that teaches that the temple will be rebuilt?"[24]

There are no explicit statements in Scripture that say, "The Jewish temple will be rebuilt." However, there are explicit statements in Scripture that require the existence of a Jewish temple during the future tribulation period. I must again point to the doctrine of the Trinity to make my point. There are no explicit statements in Scripture that say, "God is a Trinity." However, there are explicit statements in Scripture that require the doctrine of the Trinity: there is one, and only one, God; the Father is God; Jesus is God; the Holy Spirit is God; the Father, Son, and Holy Spirit are persons who are distinct from each other.

Similar to the doctrine of the Trinity, there are explicit statements in Scripture that require the existence of a newly built temple during the tribulation period. An example is Matthew 24:15-16, where Jesus declares, "When you see the abomination of desolation spoken of by the prophet Daniel, standing in the holy place (let the reader understand), then let those who are in Judea flee to the mountains." The "holy place" is in the temple. There can be no "holy place" in the end times without a Jewish temple in the end times.

A good cross-reference is 2 Thessalonians 2:4, which informs us how the holy place will be profaned: the man of lawlessness (the antichrist) "opposes and exalts himself against every so-called god or object of worship, so that he takes his seat in the temple of God, proclaiming himself to be God."

Preterists offer a different explanation of these verses that relate to the destruction of Jerusalem in AD 70, but a plain and literal reading of them requires the existence of a Jewish temple in the end times. Remember, Old Testament prophecies of the first coming of Christ were literally fulfilled. Likewise, the prophecies that deal with the second coming— and all the events in the tribulation period that lead up to that coming, including the existence of a Jewish temple—will be fulfilled literally. The precedent has been set for a literal interpretation of prophecy.

* * *

The case for pretribulationism remains strong and convincing, despite challenges from preterist interpreters. The next chapter will focus on the rapture and church history.

9

CHURCH HISTORY: FRIEND OR FOE OF PRETRIBULATIONISM?

Numerous claims have been made in recent years against pretribulationism as related to church history. Some claim pretribulationism is a recent view that was formulated by John Darby in the 1800s. Others claim Darby got it from the visions of a 15-year-old demon-possessed girl named Margaret MacDonald in 1830. Others claim he got it from the Irvingites. Still others claim that the doctrine of imminence—a key component of pretribulationism—is recent and finds no support in the early church. And still others say pretribulationism departs from the teachings of theological luminaries like Augustine, John Calvin, and Martin Luther.

What are we to make of such claims? Indeed, what do we know to be *factually accurate* about the rapture as related to church history? It is to these issues that we now turn our attention.

* * *

Preterists and posttribulationists often claim that the pretribulational view of the rapture is a recent doctrinal development formulated by John Nelson Darby in the 1800s. The doctrine allegedly has no support earlier than this time. Here is a sample of how the argument typically goes:

> Prior to [the time of Darby,] no hint of any approach to such belief can be found in any Christian literature from Polycarp down...Surely, a doctrine that finds no exponent or advocate in the whole history and literature of Christendom, for eighteen hundred years after the founding of the Church—a doctrine that was never taught by a Father or Doctor of the Church in the past—that has no standard Commentator or Professor of the Greek language in any Theological School until the middle of the Nineteenth century, to give it approval...ought to undergo careful scrutiny before it is admitted and tabulated as part of "the faith once for all delivered unto the saints."[1]

Pretribulationists grant that John Darby was a popularizer of the pretribulational rapture. However, this doctrine long preceded Darby's time, contrary to the false claims of preterist and posttrib critics. Following are a few examples from church history:

• Irenaeus was a disciple of Polycarp, who was himself a disciple of the apostle John (who wrote the book of Revelation). Irenaeus was born around AD 130 and died around AD 202. He wrote, "When in the end the Church shall be suddenly caught up from this, it is said, 'There shall be tribulation such as has not been since the beginning, neither shall be.'" Notice that "suddenly caught up" precedes the "tribulation."[2]

- *The Shepherd of Hermas*, an early Christian document that dates to the second century, alludes to a pretribulational rapture, even though it seems to require personal merit. This document speaks of "the great tribulation that is coming. If then ye prepare yourselves, and repent with all your heart, and turn to the Lord, it will be possible for you to escape it, if your heart be pure and spotless, and ye spend the rest of the days of your life in serving the Lord blamelessly."[3] Though pretribs believe this document errs in requiring merit, a pretrib rapture is strongly implied.

- *The Apocalypse of Elijah* is a third-century treatise about the end times that has been reconstructed from Greek and Coptic fragments. Heading up this reconstruction is Francis Gumerlock, a professor of historical theology at Providence Theological Seminary in Denver, Colorado. This treatise, he says, indicates that the rapture will occur before judgment falls. According to the document, the purpose of the rapture is "specifically removal from the wrath of the Antichrist and escape from the tribulation sent on the world by God in the last days."[4]

- Ephraem of Nisibis (also known as Pseudo-Ephraem) was born in AD 306 and died in AD 373. He was a theologian in the early Eastern (Byzantine) church. He expressed a pretribulational view of the rapture: "Count us worthy, Lord, of the rapture of the righteous, when they meet you the Master in the clouds, that we might not be tried by the bitter and inexorable judgment." He also said, "Watch always, praying continually, that you may be worthy to escape the tribulation…If anyone has tears and compunction, let him pray the Lord that he might be delivered from the tribulation which is about to come upon the earth, that he might not see it all, nor the beast himself, nor even hear of its terrors."[5] He further declares, "All the saints and elect of God are gathered together before the tribulation, which is to come, and are taken to the Lord, in order that they may not see at any time the confusion which overwhelms the world because of our sins."[6] Mark Hitchcock and Ed Hindson tell us that "Pseudo-Ephraem's comments prove that pretribulationism clearly existed long before Darby—in this case, more than 1,000 years earlier."[7] We might say the same about Irenaeus, *The Shepherd of Hermas*, and *The Apocalypse of Elijah*.

- Caesarius of Arles, an early sixth-century bishop in southern France, seems to have taught a pretribulational rapture. In Homily 8, he ties the phrase "come up hither" in Revelation 4:1 to the phrase "caught up in the clouds" in 1 Thessalonians 4:17.[8] Because Revelation 4:1 precedes the discussion of the tribulation period in Revelation 6–18, a pretrib rapture seems evident.

- Aspringius of Beja, a sixth-century bishop in southern Portugal, finds the rapture in Revelation 3:10, which promises: "Because you have kept my word about patient endurance, I will keep you from the hour of trial that is coming on the whole world, to try those who dwell on the earth." Aspringius tells us that God "promises that he will preserve his church in the last times, when the demon, enemy of the human race, will come to tempt those who live on the earth."[9] This implies a pretribulational rapture, in which the church is delivered from the antichrist.

Historian William Watson wrote an important book titled *Dispensationalism Before Darby*. In his research, he uncovered numerous references to the rapture from authors who lived in the sixteenth, seventeenth, and eighteenth centuries—all before the time of Darby. A few examples will suffice:

- Ephraim Huit, the founder of the first church in Connecticut in 1639, "believed the 'coming of the Son of Man in thee Cloudes' would save the elect from 'trials.' Huit explains the rapture as 'the summoning of the Elect by the sound of a trumpet...heard only by the Elect.'"[10]

- Increase Mather (1639–1723) was a prominent Puritan pastor in colonial New England. He became president of Harvard College (1685). In 1701, he published a book that spoke of a pretrib rapture: "When Christ comes, believers shall see the King...in all his glory and go with him to... Heaven...Christ assured believers it shall be thus, John 14:2...they will sit together with him in heavenly places... [later] they shall come down from Heaven...They shall be with him when he comes to Judge the World."[11]

- Author Robert Maton, in 1642, published books that contained sections on the rapture. "He emphasized his belief that the rapture of the living and the resurrection of the dead, with the ungodly 'left behind' to experience the wrath of God, would take place before Christ's coming with His saints to rule on earth. He referred to the rapture as the time when the 'elect meete the Lord in the aire.'"[12]

- Samuel Petto was an English Congregationalist who published *The Revelation Unveiled* in 1693. In this book, he distinguished the times of the rapture and the second coming, against those who hold that they are just one single event. He also wrote about how Christ would establish the millennial kingdom following His second coming.[13]

We can also point to Dr. John Gill, one of the most famous Bible commentators of the 1700s. This Calvinist theologian published his commentary on the New Testament in 1748. In his comments on 1 Thessalonians 4:15-17, Gill said Paul delivers a teaching that is "something new and extraordinary." He referred to the translation of the saints as "the rapture" and urged watchfulness because "it will be sudden, and unknown beforehand, and when least thought of and expected."[14]

In the excellent book *When the Trumpet Sounds* by general editors Thomas Ice and Timothy Demy, we learn that Gill's teaching on the rapture has the following components:

1. The Lord will descend in the air.

2. The saints will be raptured in the air to meet Him.

3. In the air Christ will stop and will be visible to all.

4. As yet He will not descend on earth, because it is not fit to receive him.

5. He will take up [the saints] with Him into the third heaven, till the general conflagration and burning of the world is over.

6. This will preserve them from that conflagration.

7. Then all the elect of God shall descend from heaven.

8. Then they shall be with Him, wherever He is

   a. first in the air, where they shall meet Him

   b. then in the third heaven, where they shall go up with Him

   c. then on earth, where they shall descend and reign with Him for a thousand years.[15]

Scholar Paul Benware, in his book *Understanding End Times Prophecy: A Comprehensive Approach*, adds even more Christians in the 1600s and 1700s who believed in a pretribulational rapture:

> Peter Jurieu, in his book *Approaching Deliverance of the Church* (1687), taught that Christ would come in the air to rapture the saints and return to heaven…prior to His coming in glory…Philip Doddridge's commentary on the New Testament (1738)…[uses] the term *rapture* and speaks of it as imminent. It is clear that these men believed that this coming would precede Christ's descent to the earth and the time of judgment. The purpose was to preserve believers from the time of judgment. James Macknight (1763) and Thomas Scott (1792) taught that the righteous would be carried to heaven, where they would be secure until the time of judgment was over.[16]

Who knows how many other documents out there refer to a pretrib rapture that have not yet been discovered and examined? The historical research is now in its infancy stage. Many more discoveries are sure to follow. Francis Gumerlock affirms, "As new [literary] finds are discovered, evangelicals are gradually becoming aware that pretribulationism has a much broader history than its articulations over the last two hundred years."[17]

Such historical literary finds are important. As Thomas Ice puts it, "We need to deal with the history of the rapture not because it is a basis for determining truth, which can be found in Scripture alone, but because these issues are often at the heart of the criticisms brought against the pretribulation view."[18]

Considering the historical evidence cited above, the alleged "novelty" of the pretribulational rapture should no longer be used as an argument against it.[19] The doctrine was believed in and cherished by Christians who lived far before the time of John Darby.

Speaking of Darby, it is worth noting that—like so many other Christians throughout church history—he came to his view of the rapture by a study of Scripture. *The Harvest Handbook of Bible Prophecy* informs us: "John Nelson Darby (1800–1882) claims to have first understood his view of the rapture as the result of personal Bible study during a convalescence stay at his sister's house from December 1826 until January 1827."[20] Pretribulationists today likewise hold to their view precisely because they believe in what Scripture plainly states.

• • •

A common claim is that the earlier a doctrine is present in church history, the more likely it is to be the correct view. Since pretribulationism allegedly came late in church history, it is likely to be the incorrect view.

I have demonstrated that, in truth, the doctrine of pretribulationism was taught much earlier in church history than previously thought. It can no longer legitimately be considered a "late doctrine" or a "novel view," based on recent discoveries—and with the full expectation that many other similar discoveries are on the near horizon. Nevertheless, because many claim pretribulationism is a late doctrine, it is beneficial to respond to the claim.

Foremost, many pretrib scholars have noted, and wisely so, that with the process of doctrinal development through the centuries, it makes sense that eschatology would become a focal point of discussion later in church history. Theologian John F. Walvoord, in his book *The Rapture Question*, wrote:

> The fact is that the development of most important doctrines took centuries, and it is not surprising that even in the twentieth century new light should be cast on our

understanding of Scripture. If the doctrine of the Trinity did not receive permanent statement until the fourth century and thereafter, beginning with the Council of Nicaea in 325, and if the doctrine of human depravity was not a settled doctrine of the church until the fifth century and after, and if such doctrines as the sufficiency of Scripture and the priesthood of the believer were not recognized until the Protestant Reformation, it is not to be wondered at that details of eschatology, always difficult, should unfold slowly. It is certainly an unwarranted generalization to require a detailed and systematic pretribulationism to be in existence from the apostolic age in order to accept the doctrine as true.[21]

The late Christian apologist Norman Geisler has suggested that the argument from church history involves the fallacy of "chronological snobbery"—wrongly arguing that truth is somehow determined by time. Bible expositor J. Dwight Pentecost says that the failure to discern a teaching of Scripture early in church history does not nullify that teaching or make it false.[22] Theologian Charles C. Ryrie agrees with Geisler and Pentecost, and argues that "the fact that something was taught in the first century does not make it right (unless taught in canonical Scripture), and the fact that something was not taught until the nineteenth century does not make it wrong, unless, of course, it is unscriptural."[23] Professor Thomas Howe puts it this way: "It is absurd to disregard a view because it was not thought of in the past. The claims of relativity physics were not thought of in the past, but that hardly disqualifies Einstein's assertions."[24]

Relevant to our discussion is that some in the early church held false doctrines, such as baptismal regeneration. This illustrates that just because a doctrine is early does not mean it is correct. Conversely, just because a doctrine is late does not mean it is incorrect.[25]

I am reminded that at the time of the Reformation, there were charges of "newness" brought against the Reformers. As Pentecost put it, "If the same line of reasoning were followed one would not accept the doctrine of justification by faith, for it was not clearly taught until the Reformation."[26] Reformer John Calvin responds to the charge of "newness" this way:

> First, by calling it "new" they do great wrong to God, whose Sacred Word does not deserve to be accused of novelty…That it has lain long unknown and buried is the fault of man's impiety. Now when it is restored to us by God's goodness, its claims to antiquity ought to be admitted at least by right of recovery.[27]

Please allow me to expand on this just a bit. Think of how things must have been during the Reformation. Martin Luther and John Calvin taught justification by faith alone. But some people got angry and responded, "We cannot accept this doctrine. It is a novel view. We must reject it because it is a recent development." But this "new" doctrine is a *biblical* doctrine. It is found in the Scriptures. Like-wise, pretribulationism should not be rejected because of its alleged newness. Pretribulationism is a *biblical* doctrine. It is found in the Scriptures. And besides, it turns out that it is not "new" after all. The evidence clearly proves otherwise.

• • •

Some critics have alleged that John Darby clandestinely stole the doctrine of the pretribulational rapture from a group called the Irvingites and then sought to pass it off as his discovery. The folly of this viewpoint does not require a lengthy answer. The single fact that collapses this claim like a house of cards is that Edward Irving and his movement *never taught pretribulationism.* The Irvingites held to "the historicist system which views the entire church age as the tribulation." Irving "taught that the second coming was synonymous with the rapture." He "believed that raptured saints would stay in heaven until the earth was renovated by fire and then return to the earth. This is hardly 'pretrib' since Irving believed that the tribulation began at least 1,500 years earlier and he did not teach a separate rapture, followed by the tribulation, culminating in the second coming."[28] This argument against the pretribulational rapture turns out to be no argument at all.

We can also observe that history now reveals that John Darby held a very low view of Edward Irving:

> Darby believed that "the positive work of the enemy" was "most manifest" in Irving's church. In 1844, he recalled how, "at least fourteen years ago", he had disputed with Irving on the matter of spiritual gifts, and later recollected being drawn into conflict with him "some four-and-thirty years ago", because of his "meddling metaphysically with the Lord's Person". Darby described Irving's doctrine of the Incarnation as "plainly wicked and evil, and contrary to God's word and Spirit". He...lamented "all poor Irving's heresies and wanderings"...He also criticized Irving's sermons on Daniel's vision of the four beasts, and his interpretation of Isaiah, which he believed demonstrated "the extreme neglect of Scripture and even prophecy itself, the hurried pursuit of an object in the mind". These are hardly the comments one would expect from a man allegedly impressed by, and indebted to, Edward Irving.[29]

• • •

Marvin Rosenthal, champion of the pre-wrath view of the rapture, wrote that the pretribulational view had a satanic origin and was unheard of before 1830: "In 1830, Satan, the 'father of lies,' gave to a fifteen-year-old girl named Margaret MacDonald a lengthy vision."[30] Pretribulationism was allegedly revealed in this vision.

I offer seven brief points in response to this allegation:

1. It seems clear that Rosenthal derived his rather uncharitable view from the questionable work of longtime anti-pretrib Dave MacPherson.[31]

2. No one has ever demonstrated from the facts of history that MacDonald influenced John Darby.[32]

3. History reveals that John Darby held his pretribulational view by January 1827. This is a full three years before Mac-Donald's "vision."[33] Even some opponents of the pretrib rapture acknowledge this. Anti-pretrib John Bray, for example, said it is "impossible for me to believe that Darby got his Pre-Tribulation Rapture teaching from Margaret Mac-Donald's vision in 1830. He was already a believer in it since 1827."[34]

4. Researcher Roy A. Huebner provides evidence that Darby's understanding of pretribulationism resulted solely from his interaction with the text of Scripture, not from anyone's vision.[35] And this interaction with Scripture took place years prior to the time of MacDonald's vision.

5. Paul R. Wilkinson, who wrote a doctoral dissertation relating to John Darby, writes, "Benjamin Wills Newton (1807-1899) commissioned John Darby to travel to Scotland to investigate claims that the Holy Spirit was being 'poured out' in Scotland, and that people were prophesying, being healed, and speaking in tongues...Based on what he heard and witnessed firsthand, Darby concluded that the utterances were

not to be attributed to the Holy Spirit."[36] In fact, Darby categorized Margaret MacDonald's utterances as "demonic."

6. Wilkinson continues, "From a careful reading of MacDonald's account, we may categorically conclude that her utterance bears no resemblance whatsoever to a pretrib Rapture. On the contrary, we may reasonably conclude that this fifteen-year-old girl was, in fact, advocating a post-tribulation Rapture, the Tribulation being 'the fiery trial which is to try us' and which will be 'for the purging and purifying of the real members of the body of Jesus.'...This is completely inconsistent with Darby's teaching, and with pretribulationism in general."[37]

7. Leading nineteenth-century Brethren scholar William Kelly understandably asked, "Can any fair mind in God's presence, if he knew no other facts, conceive a greater improbability than [John Darby] adopting the utterance of what he believed a demon as a truth of God?"[38]

Given these verifiable facts, it is unfortunate that Rosenthal claimed that pretribulationism had a satanic origin, with Darby deriving his doctrine from a 15-year-old girl's vision. Rosenthal says that those who have opposed his view "did not deal with the issues, misrepresented the facts, or attempted character assassination."[39] Some pretribs believe this accurately describes what Rosenthal himself has done in his response to pretribulationism. He appears to be guilty of the very thing he condemns in others.

* * *

An anti-pretrib video produced in the UK but also distributed in the USA claimed that Darby espoused a socially cultic mentality similar to that of Charles Taze Russell, who founded the Jehovah's

Witnesses, and Joseph Smith, the founding prophet of Mormonism.[40] The video sets a photograph of Darby in between those of Russell and Smith.

In response, I am the author of the following books:

- *The Challenge of the Cults and New Religions*

- *Find It Quick Handbook on Cults and New Religions*

- *Reasoning from the Scriptures with the Jehovah's Witnesses*

- *The 10 Most Important Things You Can Say to a Jehovah's Witness*

- *Conversations with Jehovah's Witnesses*

- *Reasoning from the Scriptures with the Mormons*

- *The 10 Most Important Things You Can Say to a Mormon*

Most people know very little about the kingdom of the cults and are therefore not in a position to challenge the "cultic mentality" claim in the anti-pretrib video. But I have extensively researched Charles Taze Russell and the Jehovah's Witnesses, as well as Joseph Smith and The Church of Jesus Christ of Latter-Day Saints. For our purposes, it is sufficient to note that this video is passing off *fiction* disguised as *fact*. Darby has been falsely accused. He does not have even the slightest connection to the cults. He sought to *expose* falsehoods, not *promote* them. My assessment is that this video represents an attempt to use the "guilt by association" tactic against pretribulationism. I will not dignify the video with any further comment.

• • •

Some critics claim that Roman Catholic Jesuit priest and theologian Francisco Ribera (1537–1591) developed a theology of the end times that is strikingly similar to that of John Nelson Darby's. However, Paul Wilkinson puts this claim to rest:

> Any claim that Protestant futurists in general, and Darby in particular, adopted and adapted Ribera's futurism is absolutely groundless. Ribera's amillennial and Augustinian theology of replacement, and the absence of a pretribulation Rapture position in his eschatology, completely separates him from Darby on a theological level. This, coupled with the "ample and varied arsenal of anti-Catholic polemic" which Darby employed...is evidence enough to destroy the artificial link critics have forged between Darby and the Jesuits.[41]

Critics also point to Roman Catholic priest Manuel Lacunza (1731–1801), who allegedly influenced Darby. Lacunza, using a pen name, wrote a book titled *The Coming of Messiah in Glory and Majesty*. Contrary to the critics, Darby never referenced Lacunza in any of his voluminous writings. It is true that Lacunza wrote about the restoration of Israel, the apostasy in the church, the times of the Gentiles, and the physical return of Christ to the earth (ideas easily derived from the Bible). Lacunza, however, was a strong advocate of Roman Catholic dogma, while Darby was strongly anti-Catholic. As well, Lacunza believed that Paul's letters to the Thessalonians were written to correct their "error...of expecting every moment the coming of the Lord." So, "Lacunza did not believe in an imminent return of the Lord Jesus Christ to catch away the Church; John Nelson Darby did."[42]

The truth is, critics are (again) attempting to construct a "guilt by association" attack against Darby and pretribulationists with an alleged connection to Jesuit priests, when in fact no such connection is proven or even likely.

● ● ●

Pretribulationists believe in an imminent rapture. This means they believe in an *any-moment* rapture. The term *imminent* means "ready to take place" or "impending." Nothing must be prophetically fulfilled before the rapture can occur.

Critics of pretribulationism, however, claim that the doctrine of imminence is a recent development in church history. They claim that no examples can be found among early believers who held to imminence.

Contrary to this claim, plenty of early Christians spoke of their belief in an imminent return of Christ. Following is a brief sampling:

- The Didache said, "Watch for your life's sake...Be ready, for ye know not the hour in which our Lord cometh" (16.1, around AD 120–150).

- Clement of Rome (around AD 35–101) said, "Speedily will He come, and not tarry."

- Ignatius of Antioch (d. AD 110) said of Christ's coming, "Be watchful, possessing a sleepless spirit."

- In the Epistle of Pseudo-Barnabas (around AD 70–130), we read, "The Day of the Lord is at hand...the Lord is near."

In the church fathers, we often see statements abounding with appeals to "watch," "wait," and "be ready" for the Lord's soon coming.[43] Posttribulationist J. Barton Payne conceded that the early Christians believed in the imminent coming of Christ: "Belief in the imminence of the return of Jesus was the uniform hope of the early church."[44]

Pretribulationist John F. Walvoord summarizes, "The central feature of pretribulationism, the doctrine of imminency, is...a prominent feature of the doctrine of the early church...The early church lived in constant expectation of the coming of the Lord for His church."[45]

We grant that there was some confusion among the church fathers. An example is how they often openly expressed belief in imminency while simultaneously expressing the belief that events of the tribulation period were impending. So, as Walvoord puts it, "At best, the situation is confused."[46] Nevertheless, the claim that imminency is not found among the early Christians is simply false, and rapture critics should stop making the claim.

* * *

Critics of pretribulationism argue against imminence by noting that certain prophecies had to be fulfilled before the rapture could occur. Perhaps the most oft-cited example relates to the coming of the Holy Spirit at Pentecost: "You will be baptized with the Holy Spirit not many days from now" (Acts 1:5). Because of this prophecy, the rapture could not occur "at any moment" until the prophecy was fulfilled.

The fatal flaw in this logic is that the essential Bible passages on the rapture came about 20 years after Pentecost (for example, 1 Thessalonians 4:13-18 was written around AD 51). By that time, the prophecy about the baptism of the Holy Spirit had obviously already been fulfilled, and therefore was no hindrance to imminency.[47]

It is hard to argue against the imminence of the rapture when one considers the collective weight of the following verses:

- 1 Corinthians 1:7: "…as you wait for the revealing of our Lord Jesus Christ."

- 1 Corinthians 16:22: "Our Lord, come!"

- Philippians 3:20: "Our citizenship is in heaven, and from it we await a Savior, the Lord Jesus Christ."

- Philippians 4:5: "The Lord is at hand."

- 1 Thessalonians 1:10: "...to wait for his Son from heaven."

- Titus 2:13: "...waiting for our blessed hope, the appearing of the glory of our great God and Savior Jesus Christ."

- Hebrews 9:28: "Christ...will appear a second time...to save those who are eagerly waiting for him."

- James 5:8: "The coming of the Lord is at hand."

- James 5:9: "The Judge is standing at the door."

- Revelation 3:11; 22:7, 12, 20: "I am coming soon."

- Revelation 22:20: "Surely I am coming soon."

None of these verses give even the slightest hint that certain prophecies must precede the rapture of the church.

* * *

Critics claim pretribs have failed to follow the lead of theological luminaries like Augustine, John Calvin, and Martin Luther regarding the rapture and Bible prophecy.

There is much to commend in the writings of men like Augustine, John Calvin, and Martin Luther. There is no way to quantify just how much of a blessing these men have been to the Christian church.

And yet, these men were not infallible human beings. This is illustrated in the fact that they changed their minds on certain issues, as is true of all human beings. Augustine, for example, was premillennial in his outlook in his early years. Later, he changed his mind in favor of amillennialism.

In the end, Augustine interpreted all Scripture—*except for prophecy*—in a natural and literal sense. He was inconsistent in how he interpreted prophecy. He accepted a literal second coming of Christ. He also held to a literal heaven and hell. In his later years, however, he concluded that the millennial kingdom—which premillennials believe to be a 1,000-year reign of Christ on earth—is not literal. Using an allegorical approach, he suggested that the church was already living in the millennium as part of the spiritual kingdom of God (amillennialism). He said Christ is even now reigning in the hearts of Christians. He denied there would ever be a literal kingdom on earth in which Christ would rule.

Augustine's view became the dominant view of the Roman Catholic Church. Reformation luminaries such as Martin Luther and John Calvin also adopted his view. Because such well-known theologians in church history accepted the allegorical method in interpreting prophecies relating to the millennial kingdom, many today have taken the same view, particularly in the Reformed Church. Many today apply the allegorical method not just to the millennium but to other aspects of Bible prophecy as well.

The primary concern of pretribulationists is this: *What does the Bible teach?* While the writings of notable Christians are worthy of study, they are not inspired and authoritative. They represent only human opinions. And human opinions can change (just as Augustine changed his mind on prophecy). Only Scripture is inspired and authoritative. Only Scripture speaks with the voice of God.

Pretribulationists arrived at their viewpoint because they believe this is what the Bible teaches, based on a literal approach to understanding Bible prophecy. The literal approach has much to commend it:

1. A literal interpretation is the standard approach for understanding the meaning of all languages.

2. The greater part of the Bible makes good sense when taken literally.

3. A literal approach allows for metaphorical or symbolic meanings when the context calls for it. This is often the

case in apocalyptic literature, such as the books of Daniel
and Revelation, which contain some symbols.

4. All metaphorical or symbolic meanings ultimately depend
   on the literal sense. I humbly suggest you put on your thinking cap as you wrap your brain around the following sentence: We would not know what is *not* literally true unless
   we first understand *what is* literally true. (You might want
   to read that sentence a few times.) To illustrate, we would
   not know that Jesus is not literally a gate (John 10:9) unless
   we first know that He is a human being (John 1:14; Galatians 4:4). Because Jesus is literally a human being, we
   know He is allegorically a gate in the sense that He is the
   means of entering into salvation.

5. The literal method is the only sane and safe check on the
   subjectively prone imaginations of human beings.

We find several confirmations of the literal method of interpretation
within the biblical text itself. Foundationally, later biblical texts take
earlier ones as literal. Exodus 20:10-11, for example, takes the creation
events in Genesis 1–2 quite literally. This is likewise the case regarding
the creation of Adam and Eve (Matthew 19:6; 1 Timothy 2:13), the
fall of Adam and his resulting death (Romans 5:12, 14), Noah's flood
(Matthew 24:38), and the accounts of Jonah (Matthew 12:40-42),
Moses (1 Corinthians 10:2-4, 11), and numerous other historical figures.

Further, more than 100 prophecies about the Messiah in the Old
Testament found literal fulfillment with the first coming of Jesus Christ.
These prophecies include that He would be from the seed of a woman
(Genesis 3:15), from the line of Seth (Genesis 4:25), a descendant of
Shem (Genesis 9:26), the offspring of Abraham (Genesis 12:3), from
the tribe of Judah (Genesis 49:10), the son of David (Jeremiah 23:5-
6), conceived of a virgin (Isaiah 7:14), born in Bethlehem (Micah 5:2),

the Messiah (Isaiah 40:3), the coming King (Zechariah 9:9), the sacrificial offering for our sins (Isaiah 53), the one pierced in His side at the cross (Zechariah 12:10), predicted to die around AD 33 (Daniel 9:24-25), and raised from the dead (Psalms 2; 16). There is nothing allegorical about these various prophecies.

I always remind students that if they want to understand how God will fulfill prophecies of the future, consider how He already fulfilled prophecies in the past. God is perfectly consistent. The prophecies of Christ's first coming found literal fulfillment. The prophecies of Christ's second coming—and the events that lead up to it—will likewise find literal fulfillment.

There are a few other observations worthy of note. First, by explicitly identifying parables (Matthew 13:3) and allegories (Galatians 4:24) within the text, the Bible shows that the ordinary meaning is literal. And by providing the interpretation of a parable, Jesus revealed there is a literal meaning behind each parable (Matthew 13:18-23).

We can also observe that Jesus rebuked Jewish leaders who did not interpret the resurrection literally. He thereby showed that the literal interpretation of the Old Testament was correct (Matthew 22:29-32; see also Psalms 2 and 16). Jesus' consistent literal interpretation of Old Testament Scripture—including prophetic Old Testament Scripture—is one of the most convincing pieces of evidence for a literal approach to Scripture.

So, with all due respect to Augustine, Martin Luther, and John Calvin, whose writings are invaluable, I do not believe they are correct to interpret end-times prophecies allegorically. I nevertheless continue to be greatly blessed by consulting their writings in other doctrinal areas.

• • •

The arguments from church history against pretribulationism are unconvincing and easily answered. The next chapter will zero in on the arguments for posttribulationism and midtribulationism.

ALTERNATIVE VIEWS OF THE RAPTURE—PART 1

I was once asked to co-teach a class on systematic theology at a mega-church. In most areas of theology, my theological beliefs were compatible with the co-teacher. But we differed significantly in the area of prophecy. He was posttrib while I am pretrib.

When it came time to cover the topic of prophecy, he taught the first class. By the end of his session, I knew we would need to have a chat. Apparently, when preparing to teach the class, he had not consulted a single pretrib book. He had consulted only a posttrib book that was brimming with long-discredited arguments against pretribulationism. A number of the "problems" he cited against the pretrib view ended up being straw man arguments. In other words, he represented pretribs as believing a particular thing, and then he argued against that particular thing, which pretribs do not, in fact, actually believe.

Long story short, I was able to communicate the truth about pretribulationism to the class, and I made every effort to handle my differences with the co-teacher in a God-honoring way. In fact, I came to see that my co-teacher was acting from ignorance and was unaware of the falsity of some of the arguments he was teaching in class. An important lesson from this experience is that we should make every effort to fairly represent opposing viewpoints.

In the present chapter, I will examine two alternative views of the rapture—posttribulationism and midtribulationism. Both claim to best explain the biblical data on the rapture. And both claim there are problems with pretribulationism.

Of course, there are some problems with every view of the rapture. I remind you that Dr. John F. Walvoord said that anyone who claims their view of the rapture has no difficulties has not studied the issue very carefully. We must pick the view we believe has the fewest difficulties. For Dr. Walvoord, that was pretribulationism. You already know this is my position as well.

· · ·

POSTTRIBULATIONISM

The posttribulational view says that Christ will rapture the church after the tribulation period at the second coming. Posttribs are quick to point out that Scripture confirms that all Christians will experience tribulation. For example, John 16:1-2 records Jesus saying to His disciples, "I have said all these things to you to keep you from falling away. They will put you out of the synagogues. Indeed, the hour is coming when whoever kills you will think he is offering service to God." Romans 12:12 exhorts believers to "be patient in tribulation." Hence, Christians should not place their hope in a pretribulational rapture. No one is exempt from experiencing tribulation.

Pretribulationists do not deny that Christians will experience tribulation in the world. However, it is critical to recognize that there is both a technical and a nontechnical use of the word *tribulation* in Scripture. The nontechnical use has to do with the trials and tribulations we all face while living on earth. This is why Jesus said, "In the world you will have tribulation. But take heart; I have overcome the world" (John 16:33). But this is different from the technical term "tribulation," which has reference to a specific seven-year period just preceding the second coming of Christ:

1. Scripture refers to a definite period of time of tribulation at the end of the age (Matthew 24:29-35; Revelation 3:10).

2. It will be of such severity that no period in history, past or future, will equal it (Matthew 24:21).

3. It will be shortened for the sake of the elect, as no flesh could survive it (Matthew 24:22).

4. It is called the time of Jacob's trouble, for it is a judgment on Messiah-rejecting Israel (Jeremiah 30:7; Daniel 12:1-4).

5. The heathen nations will also be judged for their sin and rejection of Christ (Isaiah 26:21; Revelation 6:15-17).

6. This tribulation period will last seven years (Daniel 9:24, 27).

7. This period will be so bad that people will want to hide and even die (Revelation 6:16).

8. It is from this horrific time of tribulation that the church will be delivered (1 Thessalonians 1:10; 5:9; Revelation 3:10).

• • •

Posttribs believe that while the church will go through the time of judgment prophesied in the book of Revelation, Christians will be "kept through" these trials—especially those relating to Satan's wrath. They believe Revelation 3:10 supports this idea: "Because you have kept my word about patient endurance, I will keep you from the hour of trial that is coming on the whole world, to try those who dwell on the earth." The phrase "keep you from" allegedly carries the idea of "keep you *through*." Posttribulationist George Ladd says, "The promise of Revelation 3:10 of being kept [from] *ek* the hour of trial need not be a promise of removal from the very physical presence of tribulation. It is a promise of preservation and deliverance in and through it."[1]

It is unreasonable to say Christians will be "kept through" (or kept safe from) the trials unleashed during the tribulation period. Many of the calamities that fall during the tribulation period are indiscriminate. Devastating earthquakes, for example, do not steer clear of Christians and afflict only unbelievers (Revelation 11:13). Wormwood—apparently a giant asteroid that will have a devastating impact on earth—will likewise afflict everyone, both believers and unbelievers (Revelation 8:11). Believers will hardly be "kept through" such horrific events.

Moreover, the tribulation period is *globally* characterized by wrath (Zephaniah 1:15, 18), judgment (Revelation 14:7), indignation (Isaiah 26:20-21), trial (Revelation 3:10), trouble (Jeremiah 30:7), destruction (Joel 1:15), darkness (Amos 5:18), desolation (Daniel 9:27), overturning (Isaiah 24:1-4), and punishment (Isaiah 24:20-21). No passage of Scripture can be found to alleviate to any degree whatsoever the severity of this time that will come upon the *entire* earth. No one will be exempt from experiencing the horror of the tribulation. No one will be able to hide from these judgments.

Further, the book of Revelation openly states that the Satan-empowered antichrist will be victorious over believers. Not only will Christians *not* be "kept through" the devil's wrath expressed through the antichrist, but the antichrist will overcome them. Scripture reveals that the antichrist will be "allowed to make war on the saints *and to conquer them*" (Revelation 13:7, emphasis added). A parallel verse is Daniel 7:21, where we are told that the antichrist "made war with the saints and *prevailed over them*" (emphasis added). How does the antichrist have such power? Satan empowers him: "The coming of the lawless one [the antichrist] is by the activity of Satan with all power and false signs and wonders" (2 Thessalonians 2:9, insert added). Revelation 13:2 tells us that Satan gives his power to the antichrist: "To it [the beast, or antichrist] the dragon [Satan] gave his power and his throne and great authority" (inserts added). Given such verses, we can confidently say that Christians *will not* be "kept through" the devil's wrath but will be overcome by it as it is expressed through the antichrist. Indeed, Revelation 6:9 indicates that many Christians will be martyred during the tribulation period. That hardly sounds like they are being "kept through" the tribulation period.

Still further, the primary text posttribulationists cite does not support their claim. Revelation 3:10 states, "Because you have kept my word about patient endurance, I will keep you from the hour of trial that is coming on the whole world, to try those who dwell on the earth." As I have noted elsewhere in the book, the word "from" in this verse ("I will keep you *from* the hour of trial") carries the idea of "out of" or "separated from" (Greek: *ek*) the actual time period of the tribulation. To be clear, believers are kept *out of* the time period of the tribulation, not kept *through* it. This verse is a powerful support for pretribulationism.

* * *

Revelation 20:5 tells us that following the tribulation period, believers who had died "came to life," thus participating in the "first resurrection." Posttribs say that because this is called the "first" resurrection—and because it occurred *after* the tribulation period—it is not possible for a resurrection to have occurred in connection with a rapture seven years earlier (before the tribulation period). Revelation 20:5 is thus compatible only with posttribulationism.

Pretribs agree with posttribs that Revelation 20:4-6 affirms that there will be a resurrection after the tribulation period—or, more accurately, just before the beginning of the millennial kingdom. They also agree that this event will be part of the "first resurrection." Pretribs note, however, that not all resurrections of believers happen at the same time. One resurrection of believers will occur in conjunction with the rapture before the tribulation period (1 Thessalonians 4:13-17). Another resurrection of believers will take place after the tribulation period (Revelation 20:4-6). Both are part of what Scripture calls "the first resurrection."

Let me clarify the debate for you. Posttribulationists interpret the phrase "first resurrection" as being chronological. Pretribulationists, by contrast, interpret "first resurrection" as a *type* of resurrection. More specifically, Scripture speaks of *two types* of resurrection. The first is appropriately called the "first resurrection" (Revelation 20:5), also called the "resurrection of life" (John 5:29), the "resurrection of the just" (Luke 14:14), and the "better resurrection" (Hebrews 11:35). The "second resurrection" is the last resurrection (Revelation 20:5; see also verses 6, 11-15), appropriately called the resurrection of condemnation (John 5:29; see also Daniel 12:2; Acts 24:15). In a capsule, the first resurrection is the resurrection of believers while the second resurrection is the resurrection of unbelievers.

The term "first resurrection" refers to *all* the resurrections of the righteous (see Luke 14:14; John 5:29), even though they are widely separated in time. There is one resurrection of the righteous at the rapture (before the tribulation—1 Thessalonians 4:13-17); another during the tribulation (the two witnesses—Revelation 11:3, 11); and another at the end of the tribulation (the martyred dead—Revelation 20:4-5). They all are "first" in the sense of being a part of the resurrection of believers. Accordingly, the term "first resurrection" applies to all the resurrections of the saints regardless of when they occur, including the resurrection of Christ Himself (the "firstfruits"—see 1 Corinthians 15:23).

The "second resurrection," or the last resurrection, is an awful spectacle. All the unsaved of all time will be resurrected at the end of Christ's millennial kingdom, judged at the great white throne judgment, and then cast alive into the lake of fire (Revelation 20:11-15).

Seen in this light, the term "first resurrection" in Revelation 20:4-6 does not argue against pretribulationism.

• • •

Posttribulationists say that "saints" are mentioned as being on the earth during the tribulation period (Revelation 13:7, 9; 14:12; 17:6). This must mean that the rapture has not yet occurred. Pretribulationism is thereby disproven.

Pretribulationists concede there will be saints on the earth during the tribulation period (Revelation 6:9-11). However, pretribs believe these people become believers during the tribulation period itself, after the rapture has occurred. Perhaps these people become convinced of the truth of Christianity after witnessing millions of Christians supernaturally vanish off the planet at the rapture. (Many Bibles and Christian books will be "left behind" to explain the event.) Or perhaps they become Christians as a result of the ministry of the 144,000 Jewish evangelists introduced in Revelation 7—who themselves come to faith in Christ after the rapture. It may also be that many become Christians because of the miraculous ministry of the two witnesses of Revelation 11, prophets who have the same kinds of powers as Moses and Elijah. The book of Revelation indicates that many people will respond to the gospel of the kingdom during the tribulation. Indeed, Scripture refers to them as "a great multitude" (Revelation 7:9-10). Given this, the fact that there are "saints" on the earth during the tribulation period does not constitute a proof against pretribulationism.

• • •

Posttribulationists say that because the same Greek word (*parousia*) is used to describe the rapture and the second coming, both events must occur simultaneously. The word *parousia* means "coming," "arrival," or "presence." The term is used for the rapture in 1 Thessalonians 4:15 and of the second coming in Matthew 24:27. This supposedly argues against the idea of a pretribulational rapture.

Pretribulationists grant that the Greek word *parousia* means "coming," "arrival," or "presence." However, this simply means that both the rapture and the second coming—one before the tribulation and the other after it—are characterized by the coming, arrival, and presence of Jesus Christ.

Theologian Charles Ryrie offers this illustration of how the same word can refer to two different events:

> Suppose proud grandparents should say to their friends. "We are looking forward to enjoying the presence (*parousia*) of our grandchildren next week"; then later in the conversation add, "Yes, we expect our grandchildren to be present at our golden wedding celebration." If you heard those statements, you could draw one of two conclusions. (1) The grandchildren are coming next week for the golden wedding anniversary. In other words, the grandparents were speaking of the coming and the anniversary as a single event, occurring at the same time. Or (2) the grandchildren will be making two trips to see their grandparents—one next week (perhaps as part of their vacation) and another later to help celebrate the golden wedding anniversary.[2]

Ryrie's point, of course, is that the Greek word *parousia* can refer to two separate comings of Jesus Christ—the rapture and the second coming, separated by seven years.

• • •

Posttribulationists argue that the phrase "to meet the Lord" in 1 Thessalonians 4:17 carries the idea of believers who have just been raptured going out to meet Jesus in the air and then accompanying Him back to earth. They are not taken back to heaven.

Pretribulationists believe the posttribulational scenario does not make good sense. As scholar John F. Walvoord notes, "The posttribulationists do not have a good explanation of why it is necessary for the saints to leave the earth if, as a matter of fact, Christ is coming to the earth to reign on the earth."[3] Why go meet the Lord in the air if Christians are going to come right back down to the earth with Him? Why not just wait for Him on the earth? Furthermore, 1 Thessalonians 4:13-18—the primary reference to the rapture in the New Testament—says absolutely nothing about believers meeting the Lord in the air only to accompany Him right back down to the earth.

Contrary to this interpretation, Jesus' words about the rapture in John 14:2-3 indicate He will transport believers back to heaven immediately following the rapture: "In my Father's house are many rooms. If it were not so, would I have told you that I go to prepare a place for you? And if I go and prepare a place for you, I will come again and will take you to myself, that where I am you may be also."

This verse clearly indicates that Christ "will come again and will take" believers to Himself, that they may be in the place He has prepared in His "Father's house." The Father's house refers to heaven, where there are many dwelling places. There is room there for all the redeemed.[4] This place is described in detail in Revelation 21–22. So, at the rapture, Christ will not meet believers in the air and then descend back to the earth. Rather, according to Christ's own testimony in John 14:1-3, He will meet believers in the air and then transport them back to heaven. As explained by Arnold Fruchtenbaum in his book *The Footsteps of the Messiah*: "This is a coming to take the saints *to heaven*, and not to the earth. This is important, because in posttribulationism, the saints meet the Lord in the air and return with Him to the earth. But that is not the promise here. Yeshua [Jesus] is coming to take the saints to heaven."[5]

At this juncture, we can observe that the posttribulational scenario raises a thorny problem: *Who will populate Christ's 1,000-year millennial kingdom in their mortal bodies, as Scripture clearly teaches?* Scripture says that the believers who enter the millennial kingdom will still be married, bear children, grow old, and die (see Isaiah 65:20; Matthew 25:31-46). But if all believers are raptured (and they all receive their resurrection/glorified bodies) at the second coming, then there will be no believers left to enter the millennial kingdom in their mortal bodies.

Immediately following the second coming, Christ will gather the sheep and the goats and will judge them according to how they all treated Christ's "brothers" (likely the 144,000 Jewish witnesses described in Revelation 7 and 14). At this judgment, there will be a separation of the sheep from the goats. However, if there is a posttribulational rapture, they will already have been separated. There won't be any "sheep" left to separate from the goats. As well, all the sheep will now be in their resurrected/glorified bodies, so that no mortal Christians are left on the earth. But Matthew 25:31-46 indicates that mortal Christians will enter into the millennial kingdom. Where do they come from? That is the problem for posttribulationism.[6]

This is no problem for pretribulationism, which teaches that after the rapture, many will become believers during the tribulation period. It is these Christians who will enter the millennial kingdom in their mortal bodies, following the second coming of Christ.

• • •

Posttribulationists believe Matthew 24:37-42 refers to the rapture: "Two men will be in the field; one will be taken and one left," and "two women will be grinding at the mill; one will be taken and one left." Since these "takings" are in the context of the second coming, the rapture must occur at the second coming and not before the tribulation period.

Pretribulationists deny that this passage refers to the rapture. The parallel passage in Luke 17:34-37 indicates that those who are "taken" are taken not in the rapture but in judgment. In this passage, Jesus informs His followers, "'I tell you, in that night there will be two in one bed. One will be taken and the other left. There will be two women grinding together. One will be taken and the other left.' And they said to him, 'Where, Lord?' He said to them, 'Where the corpse is, there the vultures will gather.'" So, where will they be taken? They will be taken to a place where vultures feed upon dead corpses. In other words, these people are taken away in judgment. Hence, Matthew 24:37-40 does not support a posttribulational rapture.

There are certainly other arguments posttribs cite in favor of their view. But the preceding is sufficient to give you a feel for their overall approach.

• • •

MIDTRIBULATIONISM

Midtribulationists begin with the observation that a number of prophetic passages emphasize the midpoint of the seven-year tribulation period and the severe tribulations of the last three-and-a-half years. For example, Daniel 9:27, speaking of the antichrist, says, "He shall make a strong covenant with many for one week, and for half of the week he shall put an end to sacrifice and offering." So, the antichrist will stop Jewish sacrifices in the temple at the midpoint of the tribulation. Revelation 13:5, which also speaks of the antichrist, says that "the beast was given a mouth uttering haughty and blasphemous words, and it was allowed to exercise authority for forty-two months," which is three-and-a-half years. This means the antichrist will come into great power in the second half of the tribulation period.

Things will be terrible during this second half of the tribulation. Revelation 11:2 says the holy city (Jerusalem) will be trampled for 42 months (three-and-a-half years). Revelation 12:6 indicates that the Jewish remnant will flee into the wilderness, where it will be sustained for 1,260 days (three-and-a-half years). Verse 14 continues to speak of the Jewish remnant: "The woman was given the two wings of the great eagle so that she might fly from the serpent into the wilderness, to the place where she is to be nourished for a *time*, and *times*, and *half a time*" (emphasis added). In this verse, "time" is a year, "times" is two years, and "half a time" is half a year, totaling up to three-and-a-half years.

Because prophetic Scripture often speaks of the midpoint of the tribulation period and emphasizes the great severity of the last three-and-a-half years, midtribulationists conclude that the rapture occurs then. More specifically, the rapture will occur after the "beginning of sorrows" (Matthew 24:8 NKJV), which refers to all seven seal judgments and the first six trumpet judgments of Revelation 6–9, but before the "great tribulation" (Matthew 24:21 NKJV). Midtribulationists claim that the "beginning of sorrows" is the first half of the tribulation, whereas the "great tribulation" is the second half.

Midtribulationists point to 1 Thessalonians 5:9, which specifically states that the church will be delivered from wrath (1 Thessalonians 5:9), which, they say, occurs only during the second half of the tribulation. So, in this view, the last half of the seventieth week of Daniel (Daniel 9:24-27) is much more severe than the first half. It is only this last half of the tribulation—the *great* tribulation—that the church will be delivered from (see Revelation 11:2; 12:6).

Pretribulationists respond to this viewpoint in several ways. First, they agree that the tribulation period is divided into two periods, each being three-and-a-half years. They also agree:

1. The antichrist will cause sacrifices to cease in the Jewish temple at the midpoint of the tribulation (Daniel 9:27).

2. The Jews will flee from Jerusalem into the wilderness at the midpoint of the tribulation (Revelation 12:6, 14).

3. The second half of the tribulation period will be significantly worse than the first half. (The judgments will get progressively worse.)

But here is the big problem for midtribulationism: *The rapture is nowhere mentioned—or alluded to—or even implied—at the midpoint of the tribulation period.* It is simply not there. The Bible specifies a number of events that will transpire at the midpoint of the tribulation. These include the little scroll being opened, the antichrist being wounded and then appearing to be resurrected, Satan being cast out of heaven, the false world religious system being destroyed, God's two prophetic witnesses being executed and then resurrecting from the dead, the antichrist breaking his covenant with Israel, the abomination of desolation occurring, the antichrist blaspheming God, the Jewish remnant fleeing Jerusalem, and Satan making war on the saints. And yet, while the Bible is very specific about these events that take place at the midpoint of the tribulation period, Scripture is deafeningly silent on any rapture taking place at this point. Why is this so? *Because the rapture does not occur at this time!*

There is another factor to consider here. If the midtribulationist scenario is correct, then the doctrine of the imminence of the rapture must be dismissed. A midtribulational rapture must necessarily be preceded by three-and-a-half years' worth of signs. After all, the tribulation begins when the antichrist signs a covenant with Israel (Daniel 9:27), and this would essentially begin a three-and-a-half-year countdown to the day of the rapture (at the midpoint of the tribulation). Any idea of an *any-moment* rapture is out the back door in this scenario.

Now, the doctrine of an imminent rapture is prevalent in the New Testament (see Romans 13:11-12; 1 Corinthians 1:7; 16:22; Philippians 3:20; 4:5; 1 Thessalonians 1:10; Titus 2:13; Hebrews 9:28; James 5:7-9; 1 Peter 1:13; Jude 21). The New Testament portrays the rapture as a *signless event* that can occur *at any moment.*

Ultimately, imminence makes sense only within the theology of pretribulationism. In midtribulationism, the rapture occurs three-and-a-half years into the tribulation. In posttribulationism, the rapture follows the entire seven years of the tribulation. Hence, imminency is impossible in these systems.

• • •

Midtribulationists believe that what Christians will experience during the first three-and-a-half years of the tribulation period will be difficult, just as Christians of all ages have had to suffer tribulations (see Acts 14:22; Romans 8:18; 2 Corinthians 4:17; 1 Peter 1:6). But the tribulations of this first half of Daniel's seventieth week will involve human wrath against other humans, instead of God's wrath against human beings. God's wrath allegedly does not fall until the last three-and-a-half years of the tribulation period. The church will be raptured before the wrath of God falls.

Pretribulationists respond by pointing to the scriptural teaching that God's wrath characterizes the *entire* seven-year period. Consider, for example, that Zephaniah 1:15, 18 describes the entire tribulation period as "a day of wrath" and "the day of the wrath of the LORD" (see also 1 Thessalonians 1:10; Revelation 6:17; 14:7, 10; 19:2). While midtribulationists like to say that Revelation 6–9 refers only to the beginning of sorrows, we read in Revelation 6:17 that "the great day of their wrath has come, and who can stand?" "Their wrath" refers to the wrath of the Father and the Lamb, Jesus Christ. This wrath begins in the first half of the tribulation period.

One must remember that Christ Himself is the one who opens

each of the seals in the seven seal judgments (Revelation 6), meaning that *He initiates each of these judgments.* These seal judgments are unleashed in the first half of the tribulation period. Clearly then, the wrath of God begins falling on humankind in the first half of the tribulation.

Note also that earlier in the book of Revelation, the church is promised deliverance from the "hour of trial" that is coming upon the earth (Revelation 3:10). This verse indicates that the church will not only be delivered from wrath but from the *actual time period* of God's wrath, which would mean the entire seven-year tribulation period (see also 1 Thessalonians 5:9).

Granted, there are instances in which we witness examples of what might be called the wrath of human beings in the first half of the tribulation period. However, midtribulationists seem to forget that divine wrath can be expressed through human agency. Is this not what we witness throughout biblical history? For example, God showed His displeasure against Israel in Old Testament times by having the Jews go into Babylonian captivity. The Assyrian captivity is another example. In both cases, God chastised His people through human agency. Hence, simply because we witness examples of human wrath in the first half of the tribulation period does not mean God's wrath is not being expressed. God's wrath is falling upon the world through human agency.

● ● ●

Midtribulationists declare that the two prophetic witnesses of Revelation 11—witnesses who are resurrected and then caught up to heaven—represent a midtribulational rapture. Since this event takes place at the midpoint of the tribulation, this must mean the church is raptured at this time as well.

This argument appears to be more *eisegesis* (reading a meaning into the text) than *exegesis* (deriving the meaning from the text itself).

There is virtually no indication in the text of Revelation that the two witnesses represent the church being caught up in the rapture. Scripture delineates quite a number of prophetic events that take place at the midpoint of the tribulation period (see the previous discussion). If the rapture took place at this time, it would surely be mentioned along with the other prophetic events. Such a global vanishing of countless Christians would be too momentous an event to leave out of the list of prophetic events that will take place at this time. But alas, Scripture is silent on the matter.

We know from the text of Scripture that during the tribulation period, God will raise up two mighty witnesses who will testify to the true God with astounding power. The power of these witnesses recalls Elijah (1 Kings 17; Malachi 4:5) and Moses (Exodus 7–11). It is significant that in the Old Testament, two witnesses were required to confirm testimony (see Deuteronomy 17:6; 19:15; Matthew 18:16; John 8:17; Hebrews 10:28). Hence, these two witnesses will supernaturally confirm God's truth during the tribulation period.

The two witnesses seem connected to Israel, not the church (which will be raptured). The tribulation—the seventieth week of Daniel—is a period in which God deals predominantly with the Jews, just like He did in the first 69 weeks of Daniel (see Daniel 9:26-27). Because the two witnesses seem connected to Israel, it does not make good sense to view them as representing the catching up of the church at the rapture.

There is one final point to make here. In a number of cases in the book of Revelation, symbols are defined for us in the text itself so that we do not miss the intended meaning. For example, Jesus explained that the seven stars in His right hand were "the seven angels (messengers) to the seven churches" (Revelation 1:20). He affirmed that the seven lampstands were the seven churches (1:20). The bowls of incense represent the prayers of the saints (5:8). The "many waters" symbolize "peoples and multitudes and nations and languages" (17:15). But no such textual clues are found in reference to the two witnesses of Revelation 11. There is no evidence that the ascension of these witnesses symbolizes the church or the rapture.

* * *

Midtribulationists declare that because the rapture occurs at the "last trumpet" (1 Thessalonians 4:16-17)—and because the seventh trumpet sounds at the midpoint of the tribulation period (Revelation 11:15-19)—the rapture must occur at the midpoint of the tribulation.

This may sound like a convincing argument. However, the big problem with this view is that the seventh trumpet in Revelation 11:15 sounds toward the end of the tribulation period, not at the midpoint. Hence, if one relates the trumpet in 1 Thessalonians to the one in Revelation 11, that would place the rapture toward the end of the tribulation.

Another difficulty with this view is that while the trumpet in 1 Thessalonians 4 deals with the rapture, the seventh trumpet in Revelation deals specifically with judgment, as do the other trumpet judgments. This illustrates how trumpets are used in a variety of ways in Scripture. Theologian Charles C. Ryrie observes that the midtribulational view "assumes that all blowing of trumpets must indicate the same kind of event. This is not true. In Jewish apocalyptic literature, trumpets signaled a variety of great eschatological events, including judgments, the gathering of the elect, and resurrection."[7] Hence, the trumpet argument is not valid support for midtribulationism.

* * *

In 2 Thessalonians 2:1-4, we read:

> Now concerning the coming of our Lord Jesus Christ and
> our being gathered together to him, we ask you, brothers,
> not to be quickly shaken in mind or alarmed, either by a

spirit or a spoken word, or a letter seeming to be from us, to the effect that the day of the Lord has come. Let no one deceive you in any way. For that day will not come, unless the rebellion comes first, and the man of lawlessness is revealed, the son of destruction, who opposes and exalts himself against every so-called god or object of worship, so that he takes his seat in the temple of God, proclaiming himself to be God.

Midtribulationists reason that specific signs—the "rebellion" and the rise of the "man of lawlessness" (the antichrist)—must precede the rapture of the church ("our being gathered together to him"). This passage allegedly makes the pretribulational view impossible.

Pretribulationists rebut that this is an incorrect understanding of 2 Thessalonians 2. A careful reading of the text reveals that the signs specified occur *during* the tribulation period—"the day of the Lord"—and not before the rapture.

The backdrop is that the apostle Paul had earlier taught the Thessalonian Christians that they would be raptured before the tribulation period, or "day of the Lord" (a day of the Lord's judgment). The problem was that some false teachers had come to Thessalonica and told the believers there that they were *already in* the Day of the Lord (or tribulation period). This understandably unsettled them. So, in 2 Thessalonians, the apostle clarified the matter for them. He pointed out that the major events of the tribulation period—such as the "rebellion" and the rise of the antichrist—had not yet occurred. This proves that the tribulation period had not yet started. Hence, the Thessalonians Christians should relax. They need no longer be alarmed.

The apostle Paul then emphasized that the antichrist cannot rise on the scene until "he who now restrains" is removed (2 Thessalonians 2:7). Who is this restrainer? It is apparently the Holy Spirit, who will be removed when the church is raptured off the earth. Remember that the church is the temple of the Holy Spirit (1 Corinthians 3:16; 6:19). So, when the church is raptured off the earth, the Holy Spirit will be removed too. The Holy Spirit-empowered church will no longer be around to resist the rise of evil. Then and only then will the antichrist emerge in the tribulation period. Hence, instead of arguing against pretribulationism, this passage is actually a strong support *for* pretribulationism.

* * *

As was true of posttribulationism, there are other arguments midtribs sometimes cite in favor of their view. But the preceding serves to give you a feel for their overall approach.

We have seen that the arguments offered against pretribulationism by proponents of posttribulationism and midtribulationism are easily answered. In the next chapter, I will examine the claims of prewrath proponents and partial-rapture proponents. Their claims too, are easily answered.

ALTERNATIVE VIEWS OF THE RAPTURE—PART 2

At one time, there were three primary views of the rapture—pretribulationism, midtribulationism, and posttribulationism. Another view that has gained some traction in recent decades is the pre-wrath view. One other view—the partial rapture theory—has been around for a long time, but it has not found favor with many people. In order of popularity, the five views of the rapture are:

1. pretribulationism

2. posttribulationism

3. midtribulationism

4. the pre-wrath view

5. the partial rapture view

In this chapter, I will briefly consider the pre-wrath and partial rapture views. Proponents of these positions believe their respective views best explain the biblical data. In the process of arguing for their views, they also set forth what they perceive to be weaknesses in pretribulationism.

• • •

THE PRE-WRATH VIEW

Pre-wrath proponents argue that since the word *wrath* does not appear in the book of Revelation until after the sixth seal, this must mean God's wrath will not be poured out on the earth until the seventh seal (Revelation 6:12–8:1; see also 2 Thessalonians 1:5-10). This means the rapture must take place between the sixth and seventh seals, toward the end of the tribulation period.

Pretribulationists rebut that God's wrath is poured out on the earth far before the seventh seal. Zephaniah describes the entire tribulation period this way: "The great day of the Lord is near, near and hastening fast; the sound of the day of the Lord is bitter…A day of wrath is that day, a day of distress and anguish, a day of ruin and devastation, a day of darkness and gloom, a day of clouds and thick darkness" (Zephaniah 1:14-15). Hence, the entire tribulation period is characterized by God's wrath.

In keeping with this, 1 Thessalonians 1:10 informs us that Jesus "delivers us from *the* wrath to come" (emphasis added). Notice the definite article, "the." Many believe "*the* wrath" points to a definite and specific future period of wrath. This period of wrath is most naturally understood as being the entire seven-year tribulation period, which is elsewhere called "the time of Jacob's trouble" (Jeremiah 30:7; see also Revelation 6:17; 14:7, 10; 19:2).

Scripture portrays the seven seal judgments as a sequence, all coming from the same ultimate source—God (Revelation 6; 8). This sequence features divine judgments that increase in intensity with each new seal. Both human beings and warfare are seen as instruments of God's wrath during the first six seals. Even the unsaved who experience this wrath recognize it specifically as the "wrath of the lamb" (Revelation 6:15-16). This recognition is appropriate, for Christ Himself—the Lamb of God—opens each seal that consequently causes each respective judgment (see Revelation 6:1, 3, 5, 7, 9, 12; 8:1). It therefore hardly seems feasible to suggest that God's wrath does not begin until the seventh seal. All seven seal judgments are expressions of God's wrath, and since the seal judgments begin early in the tribulation period, God's wrath falls early in the tribulation period.

Simply because the word *wrath* is not used until the seventh seal does not mean that God's wrath has not fallen before that time. Norman Geisler explains that "the word *wrath* does not appear in Genesis, yet God's wrath was poured out during the Flood (6–8) and on Sodom and Gomorrah (19)."[1] In Bible times, people often experienced God's wrath, even though the word *wrath* was not used in the biblical text.

Pre-wrath proponents attempt to rebut that during the first six seal judgments, people suffer only the *wrath of man*, not the *wrath of God*. However, again, it is Christ who opens each seal, thereby initiating each judgment on earth (see Revelation 6). Hence, this is a clear instance of God (Christ) using human agency to express His wrath. God has often done this in the past. For example, when God needed to chasten the Jewish people in Old Testament times, He sent them into captivity under both the Assyrians and the Babylonians.

Notice also that the four horsemen of the apocalypse, in fulfillment of the first four seal judgments, are all initiated by four "living creatures" who descend from the very presence of God (Revelation 4:6-8). This, too, indicates that all the seal judgments are expressions of the wrath of God.

We also notice that the kinds of judgments that are unleashed in the first four seal judgments are typical expressions of divine wrath in Bible days—the sword, famine, pestilence, and wild beasts (see Ezekiel 14:21; Leviticus 26:22, 25; Deuteronomy 28:21-25; Jeremiah 15:2-3;

16:4; Ezekiel 5:12, 17). All these facts make it untenable to suggest that God's wrath does not fall until the latter part of the tribulation period.

• • •

In a truly novel approach, Marvin Rosenthal—a major proponent of the pre-wrath view—declares that the phrase "the tribulation period" should be omitted from all discussions about the rapture. It should not be used as a synonym for the entire seventieth week of Daniel, he says, for such a phrase allegedly predisposes one to pretribulationism—the idea that the rapture will occur before any part of the tribulation begins. He claims that pretribulationists have coined a technical phrase and superimposed it onto the Scriptures.

While pretribulationists may use the phrase "the tribulation period" as a *technical* term, they use it more importantly as a *descriptive* term. After all, the seventieth week of Daniel will be a seven-year period characterized by tribulation—a period brimming over with wrath (Zephaniah 1:15, 18), judgment (Revelation 14:7), indignation (Isaiah 26:20-21), trial (Revelation 3:10), trouble (Jeremiah 30:7), destruction (Joel 1:15), darkness (Amos 5:18), desolation (Daniel 9:27), overturning (Isaiah 24:1-4), and punishment (Isaiah 24:20-21). Since the seventieth week is characterized by such intense tribulation, the term "tribulation period" is a perfectly appropriate designation for it.

Besides, posttribulationists and midtribulationists have no problem with the term. Hence, the claim that the term predisposes one toward pretribulationism is simply false.

• • •

Pre-wrath proponents divide the seventieth week of Daniel into three recognizable periods—the "Beginning of Sorrows," the "Great Tribulation," and the frequently predicted "Day of the Lord." The first three-and-a-half years are the Beginning of Sorrows. The midpoint of the seventieth week of Daniel begins the Great Tribulation, and lasts just one-and-three-fourths years (21 months). The final 21 months—the fourth quarter of the seven-year period—constitute the Day of the Lord, in which alone is found the wrath of God.

In the pre-wrath scenario, the rapture occurs just before the Day of the Lord, at the sounding of the seventh trumpet. Put another way, the rapture occurs between the end of the third quarter and the beginning of the fourth quarter of Daniel's seventieth week. This allows the church to escape the unleashing of God's wrath.

In response to this somewhat complicated scenario, Scripture reveals that the Day of the Lord is characterized by God actively intervening supernaturally to bring judgment against sin in the world. Among the New Testament writers, the term is used for the judgments that will be unleashed in the future seven-year tribulation period (2 Thessalonians 2:2; Revelation 16–18). Most prophecy experts believe the Day of the Lord is correctly placed after the rapture in conjunction with the beginning of the tribulation period.

Contrary to the pre-wrath division of the seventieth week of Daniel into three periods—the Beginning of Sorrows, the Great Tribulation, and the Day of the Lord—Scripture points to the *entire* tribulation period as constituting the Day of the Lord (Daniel 12:1; Joel 2:1-2; Matthew 24:21). During this "day" of judgment, God inflicts seal judgments, the trumpet judgments, and the bowl judgments. All of these are expressions of the wrath of God since all find their origin in God.

The seal judgments include the rise of the antichrist, the outbreak of war, widespread famine, massive casualties, a devastating earthquake, and even worse judgments (Revelation 6:1-17). Things will progressively go from bad to worse.

The trumpet judgments (Revelation 8:7–9:21) include hail and fire falling on the earth, a fiery mountain plummeting into the sea, a star (asteroid) falling from heaven and making a severe impact on the earth, various cosmic disturbances, hideous demons torturing humans, fallen angels killing a third of humankind, and even worse judgments. This will be a time of horrific suffering on earth.

Then come the bowl judgments (Revelation 16:2-21). People will suffer harmful and painful sores, the sea will become like blood, the rivers and springs of water will also become like blood, the sun will scorch people with fire, the world will plunge into utter darkness, the Euphrates River will dry up (preparing the way for the outbreak of Armageddon), and more. Woe to those who are upon the earth at this time.

All these judgments—bar none—comprise the Day of the Lord. Pre-wrath proponents, however, exempt the first six seal judgments from the Day of the Lord, categorizing these not as God's wrath but as man's wrath. But as noted previously, God's wrath is expressed *through* man's wrath in the seal judgments. Hence, the seal judgments are properly a part of the Day of the Lord.

We can also observe that some of the seal judgments are far beyond human capabilities, and therefore cannot be categorized as part of man's wrath. A case in point is that when the sixth seal was opened, "there was a great earthquake, and the sun became black as sackcloth, the full moon became like blood, and the stars of the sky fell to the earth as the fig tree sheds its winter fruit when shaken by a gale. The sky vanished like a scroll that is being rolled up, and every mountain and island was removed from its place" (Revelation 6:12-14; see also Amos 5:18-20).

* * *

In the pre-wrath view, since the rapture is placed precisely after three-quarters of the seventieth week of Daniel, Rosenthal calls the doctrine of imminence untenable. No longer can Christians look forward to the possibility of the rapture occurring at any moment.

I've made it a habit over the years to test truth claims by following the practice of the Berean Christians. They examined the scriptures daily to test what they had been taught (Acts 17:11). Testing Rosenthal's dismissal of imminence against Scripture shows his view is not supported by it. Here is a brief sampling of relevant verses:

1. The Judge is standing at the door—James 5:9.

2. The Lord's coming is near—James 5:8.

3. The Lord is at hand—Philippians 4:5.

4. Salvation is nearer now than when we first believed—Romans 13:11-12.

5. We await God's Son—1 Thessalonians 1:10.

6. We await our great God and Savior—Titus 2:13.

7. We await the revealing of the Lord—1 Corinthians 1:7.

8. We await the revelation of Jesus Christ—1 Peter 1:13.

9. We await the Savior—Philippians 3:20.

10. We eagerly await Him—Hebrews 9:28.

Notice that these verses do not exhort us to await the coming of the Beginning of Sorrows, or the Great Tribulation, or the Day of the Lord. Rather, these verses exhort us to await and eagerly anticipate the imminent coming of Jesus (which is a coming at the pretribulational rapture).

Because Scripture teaches the doctrine of imminence—and since the pre-wrath view is incompatible with the doctrine of imminence—this can only mean that the pre-wrath interpretation must be wrong. By contrast, imminence fits perfectly with pretribulationism.

• • •

THE PARTIAL RAPTURE VIEW

The partial rapture theory teaches that only those believers who are "watching" and "waiting" for the Lord's return will be found worthy to escape the trials of the tribulation by being taken in the rapture (1 Corinthians 9:27; Hebrews 9:28; Revelation 3:10). As one partial rapturist put it, this view says that "only a prepared and expectant section of believers will then be translated."[2] Indeed, "we believe that frequent exhortations in the Scriptures to watch, to be faithful, to be ready for Christ's coming, to live Spirit-filled lives, all suggest that translation is a reward."[3]

In this line of thought, unsanctified believers left behind on earth will experience a time of purging as they suffer through the trials of the tribulation period. This is viewed as necessary because sin has made them unfit to be caught up to the direct presence of Jesus Christ.

An interesting feature of partial rapturism is that there seem to be multiple raptures throughout the tribulation period. The first of the raptures will take place before the beginning of the tribulation. Only mature living saints will be translated, and only dead saints who were mature at the time of their passing will be raised at this time. Then, throughout the seven years of the tribulation period, saints who were initially unprepared for the rapture will be raptured at various intervals as they become spiritually worthy (see Revelation 7:9, 14; 11:2; 12:5). This includes watching believers who will be raptured prior to Armageddon (16:16), and those who will be raptured at the end of the tribulation.

Pretribulationists, by contrast, believe Scripture reveals that *all* who are saved—that is, *all who have placed faith in Jesus Christ for salvation* (John 3:16-17; Acts 16:31)—will participate in the rapture. Bible expositor J. Dwight Pentecost writes:

> The partial rapturist position is based on a misunderstanding of the value of the death of Christ as it frees the sinner

from condemnation and renders him acceptable to God…
The individual who has this perfect standing of Christ
can never be less than completely acceptable to God.
The partial rapturist, who insists that only those who are
"waiting" and "watching" will be translated, minimizes
the perfect standing of the child of God in Christ and
presents him before the Father in his own experimental
righteousness. The sinner, then, must be less than justified,
less than perfect in Christ.[4]

First Corinthians 15:51-52 tells us, "Behold! I tell you a mystery.
We shall not all sleep, but *we shall all be changed*, in a moment, in
the twinkling of an eye, at the last trumpet. For the trumpet will
sound, and the dead will be raised imperishable, and *we shall be
changed*" (emphasis added). Paul could not have put in any clearer.
We shall "all be changed," not "some of us will be changed," and not
"the most holy among us will be changed." Plain and simple, we will
all be changed.

When does this change take place? Not at different intervals
throughout the tribulation period, but "at the last trumpet." The fact
that "all" believers will be raptured "at the last trumpet" indicates that
they will all be raptured at the same instant.

Related to this, Scripture reveals that the Holy Spirit's baptism
places all believers into the body of Christ (1 Corinthians 12:13). No
believers are exempt from being baptized into the body of Christ,
which is the church (Romans 12:5; 1 Corinthians 10:17; 12:27; Ephesians 4:12; 5:23; Colossians 1:24; Hebrews 13:3). There is perfect
unity in the body of Christ (Ephesians 4:4). It therefore stands to
reason that all believers will be raptured (1 Thessalonians 4:16-17).
Put another way, Christ's entire body will participate in the rapture,
not just body parts (like a finger or an ear or a toe). Likewise, given
that the church is the "bride of Christ" (Ephesians 5:25-27; see also

Revelation 19:7-9; 21:1-2), it is quite clear that the entire bride of Christ—and not just part of her—will be caught up at the rapture.

Finally, notice the specific wording of 1 Thessalonians 4:13-18. At the rapture, "the dead in Christ will rise first" (verse 16). "Then we who are alive, who are left, will be caught up together with them in the clouds" (verse 17). The text does not say that "*some of* the dead in Christ will rise first," or "only the dead who had been 'watching' will rise first." Rather, it says that "the dead in Christ will rise first." This implies that *all* the dead in Christ will rise. Likewise, the text does not say, "Then some of us who are alive, who are watching and waiting, will be caught up together with them in the clouds." Rather, it says, "Then we who are alive, who are left, will be caught up together with them in the clouds." This implies that *all* living Christians will be instantly caught up to the Lord.

• • •

Partial rapturists believe the parable of the ten virgins supports their view. This parable depicts five virgins who are prepared and five who are unprepared (Matthew 25:1-13). This is interpreted to mean that only faithful and watchful Christians will be raptured. Unfaithful Christians—those who are unprepared—will be left behind to suffer through the tribulation.

Pretribulationists grant that the parable of the ten virgins depicts five virgins being prepared and five unprepared. But they deny that the parable refers to the rapture of the church. Contextually, those virgins who are unprepared refer to people—apparently unbelieving Jews—living during the tribulation period who are unprepared for Christ's second coming, seven years after the rapture. One must keep in mind that Christ's *entire* Olivet Discourse in Matthew 24 and 25 describes the tribulation period. That being so, this passage anticipates the second coming, not the rapture.

• • •

Jesus tells His followers, "Then two men will be in the field; one will be taken and one left. Two women will be grinding at the mill; one will be taken and one left. Therefore, *stay awake*, for you do not know on what day your Lord is coming" (Matthew 24:40-42, emphasis added). Partial rapturists say this verse indicates that the rapture is a reward that not all will experience. Only those who "stay awake" and watch for it will be blessed to participate in it.

I noted previously in the book that pretribulationists do not believe this passage refers to the rapture of the church. Those taken are removed not in the rapture but in judgment, to be punished. An essential cross-reference, Luke 17:35-37, clarifies this: "There will be two women grinding together. One will be taken and the other left. And they said to him, 'Where, Lord?' He said to them, 'Where the corpse is, there the vultures will gather.'" Those who are "taken" become corpses that feed the vultures. Those who are "taken" are taken in judgment. Hence, the passage does not refer to the rapture.

Besides, this passage is in the context of the tribulation period. It is found in Christ's Olivet Discourse, and as noted previously, the entire discourse describes the tribulation period. At the end of the tribulation, unbelievers will be "taken" away to judgment, while believers will be "left" to enter Christ's millennial kingdom.

• • •

Proponents of partial rapturism observe that in 1 Corinthians 9:27, Paul said, "I discipline my body and keep it under control, lest after preaching to others I myself should be disqualified." They take this to mean that some Christians will be disqualified from participating in the rapture.

Titus 2:13 refers to "waiting for our blessed hope, the appearing of the glory of our great God and Savior Jesus Christ." Partial rapturists say only those who are consistently "waiting"—maintaining a state of righteousness—will participate in the blessed hope of the rapture.

In Revelation 3:10, Jesus tells the church at Philadelphia, "Because you have kept my word about patient endurance, I will keep you from the hour of trial that is coming on the whole world, to try those who dwell on the earth." Partial rapturists say those who have not kept Christ's word will be disqualified from participating in the rapture.

Such verses allegedly indicate that the rapture is not for all Christians. Only those who prove their worthiness will be raptured.

In response, all this makes it sound like participating in the rapture depends on consistent good works. Only the qualified get raptured. Only the worthy get raptured.

One problem I see is this: *How does one know whether one has "passed the test" or not? How does one know if one is worthy? How does one know if one has done enough good works?* In this line of thinking, the rapture is no longer a "blessed hope" (Titus 2:13), for no one can be sure one will participate in the event. It is more of a "blessed perhaps."

The scriptural teaching is that all of salvation is by grace through faith (see Ephesians 2:8-9). Prophecy expert Herman Hoyt notes, "To insist that a worthy life is the procuring cause of experience in the translation [or rapture] is a subtle attack upon the whole doctrine of grace."[5]

Scripture never portrays the rapture as a reward for godly living. Rather, following the rapture, Christians will participate in the judgment seat of Christ, at which point their godly living (or lack thereof) will be assessed and rewarded (Romans 14:8-10; 1 Corinthians 3:11-15; 9:24-27). At that time, each believer's life will be examined regarding deeds done while on earth. Personal motives and intents of the heart will also be weighed. However, good works are not a condition for salvation or for participating in the rapture.

One could make a case that partial rapturism devalues the death of Christ upon the cross of Calvary. This view assumes that good works put a believer in better standing with God, making them worthy of the rapture. However, Scripture reveals that Christ paid the complete price for our redemption. He paid for every single sin. Because Christ has taken the penalty for every sin, God will not punish sinning Christians again by preventing their participation in the rapture.[6] Because of Christ's complete work of redemption upon the cross (Galatians 3:13; Hebrews 9:12; 1 Peter 1:18-19), every believer is rendered worthy to participate in the rapture.

Furthermore, if Christians that are left behind are intended to be purged via the trials of the tribulation period, does this not constitute a form of purgatory for less-than-worthy Christians? Such an idea is entirely foreign to the pages of Scripture. Hebrews 10:14 tells us that "by a single offering [Christ's death upon the cross] he has *perfected for all time* those who are being sanctified" (emphasis added, insert added for clarification). No wonder Romans 8:1 categorically states, "There is therefore now no condemnation for those who are in Christ Jesus."

There is one final point that bears mentioning. No Old Testament passage on the tribulation mentions the church (Deuteronomy 4:29-30; Jeremiah 30:4-11; Daniel 8:24-27; 12:1-2). Likewise, no New Testament passage on the tribulation mentions the church (Matthew 13:30, 39-42, 48-50; 24:15-31; 1 Thessalonians 1:9-10; 5:4-9; 2 Thessalonians 2:1-11). This includes Revelation 6–18, the most detailed description of the tribulation period in the Bible. The Scriptures simply do not portray members of the church on earth during the tribulation period who are awaiting rapture based on their becoming "worthy."

Besides, God's primary purpose for the tribulation period is to deal with unbelieving Israel. Just as Daniel's first 69 weeks of years dealt with Israel, so the seventieth week of Daniel (the tribulation period) will deal with Israel. This is why the tribulation period is referred to as the "time of Jacob's trouble" (Jeremiah 30:7). ("Jacob" is a name representative of Israel.)

God's purpose is also to deal with the unbelieving nations of the world—anti-god Gentiles who have rejected Jesus Christ (Isaiah 26:21; Revelation 6:15-17). Both Israel and these anti-god unbelievers will be on the receiving end of three sets of judgments—the seal judgments (Revelation 6:1-17), the trumpet judgments (8:7–9:21), and the bowl judgments (16:2-21).

While God is dealing with unbelieving Israel and unbelieving Gentiles during the tribulation period, the church will be entirely absent because there is no reason for her to be there. All her sins have been paid for by Christ, and therefore there is no need for her to be purged (Hebrews 10:14). That is why the church will be delivered from the wrath to come (1 Thessalonians 1:10; 5:9; see also Romans 5:9).

• • •

I do not doubt the sincerity of those who hold to these alternative viewpoints. And I believe that their goal is to be biblical. All things considered, however, I believe the pretribulational view best satisfies the biblical data. In the next chapter, I will set forth the biblical case for the pretribulational rapture.

THE BIBLICAL CASE FOR THE PRETRIBULATIONAL RAPTURE

If there's one thing we've seen in this book, over and over again, it is that the doctrine of the rapture has generated significant debate—sometimes heated controversy—through the years:

- Some say the rapture will occur at the midpoint of the tribulation period.

- Some say it will happen after the tribulation.

- Some say it will occur three-fourths of the way through the tribulation.

- Some say only watchful believers will be raptured.

- Some say that because the word *rapture* is not in the Bible, the doctrine should not be believed.

- Some say the doctrine did not emerge until late in church history, and hence should not be believed.

- Some say that because the early church fathers did not hold to a pretrib rapture, neither should we.

- Some say the idea came from a 15-year-old demon-possessed girl.

I have adequately demonstrated the falsity of all these claims. In what follows, I will present a positive case for a pretribulational rapture. My hope and prayer is that all prophecy enthusiasts—regardless of one's persuasion on the timing of the rapture—will at least come to appreciate that there is a solid biblical case for a pretribulational rapture. In my humble opinion, the pretrib view makes the best sense of the biblical data.

As a preface, some arguments for a pretribulational rapture have already been cited in various chapters of the book. For example, in the course of answering some of the claims of midtribulationists and posttribulationists, I necessarily had to present some arguments for a pretribulational rapture. But it is helpful to put all positive arguments for a pretrib rapture into a single chapter, which is what I've done here. In considering the pretribulational rapture, one must not only answer objections to it (as I have done throughout this book), but also set forth a positive case for it. Any repetition is actually a good thing—it will help you remember what is important!

To review, the rapture is that glorious event in which the dead in Christ will be resurrected and living Christians will be instantly translated into their glorified bodies—and both groups will be caught up to meet Christ in the air and taken back to heaven (John 14:1-3; 1 Corinthians 15:51-54; 1 Thessalonians 4:13-17). This means there will be one generation of Christians who will never pass through death's door. They will be alive on earth one moment; the next moment, they will be instantly translated into their resurrection bodies and caught up to meet Christ in the air. What a remarkable moment that will be!

There are fascinating examples in Scripture of people being "snatched up"—often from earth to heaven. (Pay special attention to the italicized words in the following verses.) "Enoch walked with God, and he was not, for *God took him*" (Genesis 5:24). "Enoch was *taken up* so that he should not see death, and he was not found, because *God had taken him*" (Hebrews 11:5). "Elijah *went up* by a whirlwind into heaven" (2 Kings 2:11). Jesus "was *taken up*" and "*lifted up*" in the ascension (Acts 1:2, 9). Jesus' ascension is metaphorically described in Revelation 12:5 as a male child who "was *caught up* to God." We read that "the Spirit of the Lord *carried Philip away*" (Acts 8:29). The apostle Paul was "*caught up* to the third heaven" (2 Corinthians 12:2). These illustrations of being taken up or caught up illustrate that the concept of a rapture is biblical.[1] The only difference will be that the rapture will involve the taking up of countless Christians instead of just a single believer.

FIVE STAGES OF THE RAPTURE

In 1 Thessalonians 4:13-17, the apostle Paul writes:

> We do not want you to be uninformed, brothers, about those who are asleep, that you may not grieve as others do who have no hope. For since we believe that Jesus died and rose again, even so, through Jesus, God will bring with him those who have fallen asleep. For this we declare to you by a word from the Lord, that we who are alive, who are left until the coming of the Lord, will not precede those who have fallen asleep. For the Lord himself will descend from heaven with a cry of command, with the voice of an archangel, and with the sound of the trumpet of God. And the dead in Christ will rise first. Then we who are alive, who are left, will be caught up together with them in the clouds to meet the Lord in the air, and so we will always be with the Lord.

Based upon this verse, my late friend and colleague Ed Hindson observes that there are five stages to the rapture:

1. The Lord Himself will descend from heaven with a shout and with the sound of a trumpet.

2. The dead in Christ will rise first.

3. Then, we who are alive and remain on the earth will be caught up together with them in the clouds.

4. We will all meet the Lord in the air.

5. And, we will always be with Him.[2]

How wonderful that day will be!

REVELATION 3:10: BELIEVERS WILL BE KEPT FROM THE "HOUR OF TRIAL"

In Revelation 3:10, God promised the church in Philadelphia, "I will keep you from the hour of trial that is coming on the whole world, to try those who dwell on the earth." While the seven churches in Revelation 2 and 3 were historical churches in Asia Minor, Christ's words to each of these churches were intended not only for them but for all other Christians as well. We know this because following Christ's specific instructions to each church, Christ says, "He who has an ear, let him hear what the Spirit says to the churches." Notice the plural term "the churches." I believe Christ's words have relevance to every church throughout history.

Notice also the definite article ("the") before the word "hour" in Revelation 3:10 ("*the* hour of trial"). Definite articles, in the Greek language, can indicate *specificity*. As related to Revelation 3:10, the definite article seems to point to a *specific* time period, not just any "hour of testing." Contextually, it appears that it is a reference to the future tribulation period, which will be a seven-year "hour of trial." This period is described in detail in Revelation 6–18. It is from *this* period of trial that the church is to be kept.

This verse reveals that church saints will be kept from the actual time period of testing, not just the testing itself. As noted previously in the book, the Greek preposition *ek*, translated "from" in this verse ("I will keep you *from* the hour of trial"), carries the idea of separation from something. This means that believers will be kept from the hour of testing in the sense that they will be completely separated from it by being raptured before the period even begins.

Renald Showers, in his helpful book *Maranatha: Our Lord Come!*, suggests that "the language in Jesus' reference to this future period of worldwide testing implied that it was well-known to the church saints. It was well-known because both Old and New Testament Scriptures, written years before Revelation, foretold this unique, future period of testing or Tribulation, which would take place prior to the coming of the Messiah to rule the world in the Messianic Age or Millennium (Isa. 2:10-21; Dan. 12:1; Zeph. 1:14-18; Mt. 24:4-31)."[3]

That Revelation 3:10 refers to a rapture before this future period of worldwide testing is implied in verse 11: "I am coming soon. Hold fast what you have, so that no one may seize your crown." The phrase "I am coming soon" apparently refers to the imminence of the rapture, while the word "crown" refers to the rewards believers will receive at the judgment seat of Christ, which follows the rapture (1 Corinthians 9:25; 2 Timothy 4:8; James 1:12; 1 Peter 5:4; Revelation 2:10).[4]

Posttribulationists rebut that the church will be "kept through" the tribulation period. In response, one should pay particular attention to the indiscriminate nature of the judgments of the tribulation period. "The character of the judgments that will fall is such that they will affect everyone—famine, pestilence, sword, earthquake, stars falling from heaven. The only way one could be kept from that day of wrath would be to be delivered beforehand."[5] As John F. Walvoord put it, "The promise was to be kept from 'the hour' of trial, not just the trials in the hour."[6]

Notice also that this verse promises that only *church saints* will be kept out of this hour of trial coming upon the entire earth. Those who become believers during the hour of trial itself—what we might call *tribulation saints*—will suffer through the remainder of the tribulation. As Bible prophecy expert Arnold Fruchtenbaum put it in his book *The Footsteps of the Messiah*:

> Throughout the Tribulation, saints are being killed on a massive scale (Rev. 6:9-11; 11:7; 12:11; 13:7, 15; 14:13; 17:6; 18:24). If these saints are *Church saints*, they are not being kept safe and Revelation 3:10 is meaningless. Only if *Church saints* and *Tribulation saints* are kept distinct does the promise of Revelation 3:10 make any sense.[7]

THE CHURCH IS ABSENT FROM ALL TRIBULATION PASSAGES

No Old Testament passage on the tribulation period mentions the church (for example, Deuteronomy 4:29-30; Jeremiah 30:4-11; Daniel 8:24-27; 12:1-2). Likewise, no New Testament passage on the tribulation mentions the church (for example, Matthew 13:30, 39-42, 48-50; 24:15-31; 1 Thessalonians 1:9-10; 5:4-9; 2 Thessalonians 2:1-11). The church is not mentioned because the church won't be present on earth in the tribulation period.

In keeping with this, the word "church(es)" is used 19 times in the first three chapters of Revelation. However, in the section dealing with the tribulation—chapters 6 through 18—not a single mention is made of the church. The church is then mentioned once again in Revelation 22:16, where John addresses the first-century church. Why isn't the church mentioned in Revelation 6–18? *Because the church isn't there!*

Further, a pretribulational rapture best explains the massive apostasy that will engulf the world following the removal of "he who now restrains"—apparently the Holy Spirit who indwells the church (2 Thessalonians 2:3-7). Because the Holy Spirit indwells all believers (John 14:16; 1 Corinthians 3:17), He will essentially be "removed" when the church is removed at the rapture, thus making possible the fast eruption of apostasy throughout the world. Keep in mind that the Holy Spirit is the "spirit of truth" (1 Timothy 3:15; John 14:17; 15:26; 16:13). When He is removed from the earth at the rapture, *un*truth (or apostasy) will escalate dramatically.

THE CHURCH WILL BE DELIVERED FROM THE WRATH TO COME

Scripture promises that the church is not appointed to wrath (Romans 5:9; 1 Thessalonians 1:9, 10; 5:9). This means that the church cannot go through the "great day of wrath" in the tribulation period (Revelation 6:17; 14:10, 19; 15:1, 7; 16:1).

First Thessalonians 1:10 explicitly promises that Jesus "delivers us from the wrath to come." The word "delivers" in the original Greek text means "to draw or snatch out to oneself, to rescue, to save, to preserve." Greek scholar Marvin Vincent, author of *Word Studies in the New Testament*, says the verb means "to draw to oneself" and "almost invariably" refers to deliverance from "some evil or danger or enemy."[8] Indeed, Bible scholar D. Edmond Hiebert notes that "the word deliver (*rhuomai*) carries with it the idea of rescuing from something by a forcible act. The word puts an emphasis on the greatness of the peril from which deliverance is given by a mighty act of power."[9] This clearly seems to be referring to the rapture of the church before the great peril of the tribulation period.

The "snatching up" in 1 Thessalonians 1:10 sounds amazingly like the description of the rapture in 1 Thessalonians 4:16-17: "For the Lord himself will descend from heaven with a cry of command, with the voice of an archangel, and with the sound of the trumpet of God. And the dead in Christ will rise first. Then we who are alive, who are left, will be *caught up* together with them in the clouds to meet the Lord in the air, and so we will always be with the Lord" (emphasis added). The phrase "caught up" here literally means "snatch up or take away." And in both 1 Thessalonians 1:10 and 4:16-17, it is Jesus who does the snatching. So, Jesus—our Savior and Deliverer—rescues us from the wrath to come.

The Greek preposition *ek* ("from") is used in 1 Thessalonians 1:10 ("delivers us *from* the wrath to come"), just as it is used in Revelation 3:10. The term carries the idea of "separation from something." Believers will be delivered from this wrath by being completely separated from it, and it will take place via "snatching" at the rapture.

GOD HAS SET A PRECEDENT FOR RESCUING HIS PEOPLE BEFORE JUDGMENT FALLS

Throughout Scripture, God protects His people before His judgments fall (see 2 Peter 2:5-9). Here are some examples:

- Enoch was transferred to heaven before the judgment of the flood.

- Noah and his family were in the ark before the judgment of the flood.

- Lot was taken out of Sodom before judgment was poured out on Sodom and Gomorrah.

- The blood of the Paschal lamb sheltered the firstborn among the Hebrews in Egypt before judgment fell.

- The spies were safely out of Jericho and Rahab was secured before judgment fell on Jericho.

So too will the church be secured safely—via the rapture—before judgment falls in the tribulation period. It seems to be God's modus operandi to rescue His people before His judgment falls on unbelievers.

PROPHETIC PARALLELS

There are some interesting parallel teachings on the rapture in the pages of Scripture. First Thessalonians 5:9-11, for example, has parallel teachings with the most famous rapture passage, 1 Thessalonians 4:15-18. First, read through the passages, and pay special attention to the parallel words that are italicized, underlined, in bold, or in ALL CAPS:

> **1 Thessalonians 5:9-11**—"God has not destined us for wrath, but to obtain salvation through our Lord Jesus Christ, who died for us so that whether we are <u>awake</u> *or asleep* we might **live with him.** Therefore ENCOURAGE ONE ANOTHER and build one another up, just as you are doing."

> **1 Thessalonians 4:15-18**—"We who are alive, who are left until the coming of the Lord, will not precede those who have *fallen asleep.* For the Lord himself will descend from heaven with a cry of command, with the voice of an archangel, and with the sound of the trumpet of God. And the dead in Christ will rise first. Then <u>we who are alive</u>, who are left, will be caught up together with them in the clouds to meet the Lord in the air, and so we will always **be with the Lord.** Therefore ENCOURAGE ONE ANOTHER with these words."

Notice the parallels in terminology:

- The reference to "those who have fallen asleep" in 1 Thessalonians 4:15 parallels those who are "asleep" in 1 Thessalonians 5:10.

- "We who are alive" in 1 Thessalonians 4:15 parallels those who are "awake" in 1 Thessalonians 5:10 (as opposed to "sleeping" in death).

- "With the Lord" in 1 Thessalonians 4:17 parallels believers who "live with him" in 1 Thessalonians 5:10.

- "Encourage one another with these words" in 1 Thessalonians 4:18 parallels "encourage one another and build one another up" in 1 Thessalonians 5:11.

We can infer that 1 Thessalonians 5:10-11 refers to the rapture, just as 1 Thessalonians 4:15-18 does.

There are also parallels between 1 Thessalonians 4:13-18 and Jesus' description of the rapture in John 14:1-3. For example:

- John 14:3 depicts Jesus as coming again to earth, which necessarily means He will descend from the heavenly realm. Likewise, 1 Thessalonians 4:16 says Christ "will descend from heaven."

- In John 14:3, Jesus says to believers that He "will take you to myself." First Thessalonians 4:17 reveals that believers will be "caught up" to Christ.

- John 14:3 reveals that believers will be with Christ ("where I am"). First Thessalonians 4:17 affirms that believers "will always be with the Lord."

- John 14:1 contextually reveals that the purpose of this revelation about the rapture is that the hearts of Christ's followers will not be troubled. Likewise, 1 Thessalonians 4:13, 18 reveals that the purpose of this revelation about the rapture is to minimize grief and bring encouragement to God's people.

Given such similarities, it seems clear that both passages are referring to the same event—the rapture of the church. Of course, we
should not be surprised that all these passages agree. After all, the
same Holy Spirit—the "Spirit of truth"—inspired them all (2 Timothy 3:16; 2 Peter 1:21).

THE "DEPARTURE" COMES FIRST

Second Thessalonians 2:3 tells us: "Let no one deceive you in any
way. For that day will not come, unless *the rebellion* comes first, and
the man of lawlessness is revealed, the son of destruction." Notice
that I italicized "the rebellion" in this verse. Other translations render the Greek term as "apostasy": "Don't let anyone deceive you in
any way. For that day will not come unless *the apostasy* comes first
and the man of lawlessness is revealed, the man doomed to destruction" (CSB).

Bible scholars E. Schuyler English, Andy Woods, and Wayne House,
among many others, have raised the possibility that yet another translation may be preferable here: "Let no one deceive you in any way.
For that day will not come, *unless the departure comes first*, and the
man of lawlessness is revealed, the son of destruction." If this translation is correct, then the statement that "the departure comes first"
is strong evidence for pretribulationism.

The evidence for this view is substantial. English writes, "The word
[translated 'departure'] is derived from the verb *aphistemi*, used fif-
teen times in the New Testament with only three of the references
relating to religious departure [apostasy]. In eleven of the instances
the word *depart* is a good translation." In fact, "a number of ancient
versions such as Tyndale's, the Coverdale Bible, the version by Cran-
mer, the Geneva Bible, and Beza's translation, all from the sixteenth
century, render the term 'departing.'"[10] English thus concludes that
"if this translation be admitted, it would constitute an explicit statement that the rapture of the church occurs before the Tribulation."[11]

In my studied opinion, I would say this rendering is a definite possibility that is worthy of further consideration. Those desiring to study this issue in greater detail may wish to consult the short book *The Falling Away: Spiritual Departure or Physical Rapture?* by Andy Woods.

THE RAPTURE AND THE SECOND COMING DISTINGUISHED

The rapture and the second coming are different events. No prophetic signs precede the rapture, whereas the second coming is preceded by seven years of prophetic signs during the tribulation period. The rapture occurs just prior to the tribulation period, while the second coming occurs just prior to the millennial kingdom.

The pretribulational rapture involves Christ coming *for* His saints in the air before the tribulation, whereas at the second coming He will come back *with* His saints to the earth to reign for 1,000 years (Revelation 19; 20:1-6). The fact that Christ comes "with" His "holy ones" (redeemed believers) at the second coming presumes they have been previously raptured. In other words, Christ cannot come from heaven to earth *with* them (at the second coming) until He has first come to earth *for* them (at the rapture).

Moreover, every eye will see Jesus at the second coming (Revelation 1:7), but the rapture is never described as visible to the whole world. At the rapture, Christians meet Jesus in the air (1 Thessalonians 4:13-17), whereas at the second coming, Jesus' feet descend and touch the Mount of Olives (Zechariah 14:4). At the rapture, Christians are taken and unbelievers are left behind (1 Thessalonians 4:13-17); at the second coming, unbelievers are taken away in judgment (Luke 17:34-36) and mortal believers remain to enter Christ's millennial kingdom (Matthew 25:31-46).

At the rapture, Jesus will receive His bride; at the second coming, He will execute judgment (Matthew 25:31-46). The rapture will occur in the blink of an eye (1 Corinthians 15:52); the second coming will be more drawn out—long enough for the antichrist to gather his forces to battle with Christ (Revelation 19:19).

Following the rapture, believers are judged at the judgment seat of Christ (2 Corinthians 5:10); at the second coming, the nations are judged (the "sheep" and the "goats"—Matthew 25:31-46). Bible verses about the rapture bring a message of comfort (1 Thessalonians 5:18); Bible verses about the second coming are accompanied by a message of judgment (Revelation 19:15-16).

The second coming is described in detail in Revelation 19:11-16. Some pretribs suggest that if the rapture happens in conjunction with the second coming, wouldn't the text of Revelation 19:11-16 say so? Yet, there is no mention of believers being "caught up" to meet the Lord at the second coming. This may be an argument from silence, but it is nevertheless a compelling argument against posttribulationism. As one pretribulationist put it:

> If details like the casting of the beast and the false prophet into the lake of fire are mentioned, and the specific resurrection of the tribulation saints is described, how much more the Rapture and translation of the church as a whole should have been included if, as a matter of fact, it is part of this great event. Revelation 19–20 constitutes the major problem of posttribulationists. They have no scriptural proof for a posttribulational Rapture in the very passages that ought to include it.[12]

CONTRASTING THE RAPTURE AND THE SECOND COMING[13]

THE RAPTURE OF THE CHURCH	THE SECOND COMING
1. Christ comes for believers in the air.	1. Christ comes with believers to the earth.
2. All Christians on earth are translated into new bodies.	2. There is no translation of bodies.
3. Christians are taken to the Father's house in heaven.	3. Resurrected saints remain on the earth.
4. There is no judgment upon the earth.	4. Christ judges the inhabitants of the earth.
5. The church will be taken to heaven.	5. Christ sets up His kingdom on earth.
6. It could occur at any time (it is imminent).	6. It cannot occur until the end of the seven-year tribulation period.
7. There are no signs preceding it.	7. There are numerous signs preceding it.
8. It affects only believers.	8. It affects all humanity.
9. It is a time of joy.	9. It is a time of mourning.
10. It occurs before the "day of wrath."	10. It occurs after the "day of wrath."
11. Following the rapture, Satan is not bound but wreaks havoc on the earth.	11. Following the second coming, Satan is bound in the abyss for 1,000 years.
12. Christians will be judged at the judgment seat of Christ after the rapture.	12. Christians have already been judged at the judgment seat of Christ.
13. Following the rapture, the marriage of the Lamb takes place.	13. The marriage of the Lamb has already taken place.
14. Only Christ's own will see Him.	14. All those on earth will see Him.
15. The seven-year tribulation follows.	15. The 1,000-year millennium follows.

THE RAPTURE IS A "MYSTERY"

In 1 Corinthians 15:51-55, we read:

> Behold! I tell you a mystery. We shall not all sleep, but we shall all be changed, in a moment, in the twinkling of an eye, at the last trumpet. For the trumpet will sound, and the dead will be raised imperishable, and we shall be changed. For this perishable body must put on the imperishable, and this mortal body must put on immortality. When the perishable puts on the imperishable, and the mortal puts on immortality, then shall come to pass the saying that is written: "Death is swallowed up in victory." "O death, where is your victory? O death, where is your sting?"

Notice that the rapture is called a "mystery" in this passage. In the biblical sense, a mystery is a truth that was unknown to people living during Old Testament times but was revealed during New Testament times (Matthew 13:17; Colossians 1:26). While the concept of resurrection is occasionally found in the Old Testament (Psalm 16:10; Daniel 12:2), the idea of a rapture (involving the translation of the mortal bodies of living Christians into their glorified bodies) is entirely foreign to its pages. The rapture is strictly a New Testament revelation.

THE RAPTURE WILL OCCUR IN THE TWINKLING OF AN EYE

In 1 Corinthians 15:51-52, the apostle Paul describes the rapture as occurring "in the twinkling of an eye." This phrase is Paul's way of illustrating how brief the moment of the rapture will be. The fluttering of an eyelid, the blinking of an eye, is exceedingly fast.

This means the bodily transformation that living believers will experience at the rapture will be nearly instantaneous. One moment they will be on earth in mortal bodies, and the next moment they

will meet Christ in the clouds, instantly transformed into their glorified resurrection bodies.

THE BRIDE/BRIDEGROOM METAPHOR

In Scripture, Christ is portrayed as the Bridegroom (John 3:29),
while the church is described as the bride of Christ (Revelation 19:7).
The backdrop to this imagery is rooted in ancient Hebrew wedding
traditions. There were three phases:

1. The marriage was legally consummated by the parents of
   the bride and groom, after which the groom went to prepare a place for the couple to live in his father's house.

2. The bridegroom came to claim his bride.

3. There was a marriage supper—a feast lasting several days.

*All three of these phases are seen in Christ's relationship to the church,
or bride of Christ:*

1. As individuals living during the church age come to salvation
   under the Father's loving and sovereign hand, they become
   a part of the bride of Christ (or the church). Meanwhile,
   Christ the Bridegroom is in heaven, preparing a place for
   the bride of Christ to live in His Father's house (heaven).

2. The Bridegroom (Jesus Christ) comes to claim His bride at the
   rapture, at which time He takes His bride to heaven, where
   He has prepared a place (John 14:1-3). The marriage occurs
   in heaven before the second coming (Revelation 19:11-16).

3. The marriage supper of the Lamb will follow the second
   coming before Christ's institution of the millennial kingdom
   (see Daniel 12:11; compare with Matthew 22:1-14; 25:1-13).

There are other parallels as well:

- Just as ancient Jewish grooms would pay a purchase price to establish the marriage covenant, so Jesus paid a purchase price for the church (1 Corinthians 6:19-20; Acts 20:28).

- Just as a Jewish bride was declared "sanctified" or set apart in waiting for her groom, so the church is declared sanctified and set apart for Christ the Bridegroom (Ephesians 5:25-27; 1 Corinthians 1:2; 6:11; Hebrews 10:10; 13:12).

- Just as a Jewish bride was unaware of the exact time her groom would come for her, so the church is unaware of the exact time that Jesus the Bridegroom will come at the rapture, though it is an imminent event. It could happen at any time.

THE RAPTURE IS A "BLESSED HOPE"

In Scripture, the term "blessed hope" is a reference to the rapture of the church (Titus 2:13). Notice that the verse does not say Christians are "waiting for the wrath of God to be poured out during the tribulation period." Rather, it says we are "waiting for our blessed hope, the appearing of the glory of our great God and Savior Jesus Christ." In their book *Can We Still Believe in the Rapture?*, Mark Hitchcock and Ed Hindson ask, "What purpose does it serve for Jesus to batter and brutalize His bride before He comes to rescue her?"[14] What kind of blessed hope would that be?

The rapture is "blessed" in the sense that it brings blessing and a state of blessedness to believers. "Blessed hope" carries the idea of "joyous hope" or "happy hope."[15] Believers can hardly wait for it to happen! What a blessing the rapture will be!

At the rapture, the dead in Christ will be resurrected while believers still alive on earth will be instantly translated into their glorified bodies (see Romans 8:22-23; 1 Corinthians 15:51-58; Philippians

3:20-21; 1 Thessalonians 4:13-18; 1 John 3:2-3). These bodies will never again be subject to sickness, pain, or death. And we will have uninterrupted fellowship with God and our Christian loved ones. As we continue to live in this fallen world as pilgrims just passing through, we are empowered and encouraged by this magnificent hope.

Philippians 3:20-21 assures us that "our citizenship is in heaven, and from it we await a Savior, the Lord Jesus Christ, who will *transform* our lowly body to be like his glorious body" (emphasis added). The word "transform" can mean to "alter the schematics." When we are transformed into our glorified bodies, the actual schematics of our bodies will be changed so they will be fit for eternity.[16]

Notice that the "blessed hope" in Titus 2:13 strongly implies the imminence of the rapture:

> The fact that in Titus 2:13 Paul exhorts believers to look for the rapture as the blessed (happy) hope (confident expectation) for the church, without any mention of preceding signs or tribulation, strongly implies the imminence of this event—that it can occur at any time. The exhortation to watch or look for what is the hope *par excellence* of the church loses its significance if it may not arrive at any moment.[17]

THE RAPTURE IS IMMINENT

The term *imminent* means "ready to take place" or "impending." The New Testament teaches that the rapture is imminent—that is, there is nothing that must be prophetically fulfilled before the rapture occurs (see 1 Corinthians 1:7; 16:22; Philippians 3:20; 4:5; 1 Thessalonians 1:10; Titus 2:13; Hebrews 9:28; James 5:7-9; 1 Peter 1:13; Jude 21). The rapture is a signless event that can occur at any moment. This contrasts with the second coming of Christ, which is preceded by seven years of signs in the tribulation period (Revelation 6–18).

Earlier in this book, I have quoted bits and pieces of Bible verses that teach imminency. Please indulge me for a bit of redundancy in quoting more significant portions of these important Bible passages.

The imminence of the rapture is certainly implied in the apostle Paul's words in Romans 13:11-12:

> You know the time, that the hour has come for you to wake from sleep. For *salvation is nearer to us now than when we first believed.* The night is far gone; the day is at hand. So then let us cast off the works of darkness and put on the armor of light (emphasis added).

The word "salvation," in this context, must be eschatological, referring to the rapture, for this salvation is a specific future event referenced by Paul. At the end of each day, the Christian is that much closer to the time when the rapture may occur. The passage could hardly be referring to the second coming because Paul says "the day is at hand," something he would not have said if we had to pass through seven years of tribulation (with seven years' worth of signs) before the second coming could occur.

The imminency of the rapture is also implied in James 5:7-9:

> Be patient, therefore, brothers, until the coming of the Lord. See how the farmer waits for the precious fruit of the earth, being patient about it, until it receives the early and the late rains. You also, be patient. Establish your hearts, for *the coming of the Lord is at hand.* Do not grumble against one another, brothers, so that you may not be judged; behold, *the Judge is standing at the door* (emphasis added).

This passage could hardly be referring to the second coming because we are told that "the coming of the Lord is at hand" and "the Judge is standing at the door." These verses perfectly fit a pretribulational rapture, but not a second coming that will occur after seven years of woeful tribulation (and seven years' worth of signs).

When James writes of Christ as an approaching Judge (James 5:9), he is not referring to a judgment of our eternal destiny. Rather, he is writing about the judgment seat of Christ, before which every Christian will appear following the rapture: "We must all appear before the judgment seat of Christ, so that each one may receive what is due for what he has done in the body, whether good or evil" (2 Corinthians 5:10).

The truth is that imminence makes sense only within the theology of pretribulationism. In midtribulationism, the rapture takes place three-and-a-half years after the tribulation begins. In posttribulationism, the rapture follows the tribulation. Hence, imminence is impossible in these systems.

The fact that the rapture is a signless event, and could occur at any moment, ought to spur the Christian to live in purity and righteousness (see Titus 2:13-14). As one prophecy scholar put it, "The fact that the glorified, holy Son of God could step through the door of heaven at any moment is intended by God to be the most pressing, incessant motivation for holy living and aggressive ministry (including missions, evangelism, and Bible teaching) and the greatest cure for lethargy and apathy. It should make a difference in every Christian's values, actions, priorities, and goals."[18]

THE ENCOURAGEMENT OF THE RAPTURE DOES NOT MAKE SENSE IN THE POSTTRIBULATIONAL VIEW

The apostle Paul describes the rapture in detail in 1 Thessalonians 4:13-17. Paul then concludes his explanation of the rapture in verse 18 by saying, "Therefore encourage one another with these words."

This encouragement does not make good sense in the posttribulational scenario. Indeed, in posttribulationism, the verse would amount to saying, "You're going to suffer through persecution under the antichrist. You will be afflicted by three sets of judgments—the seal judgments, the trumpet judgments, and the bowl judgments. Many of you will become martyrs. You will also suffer through Armageddon. Therefore encourage one another with these words."

This exhortation to encouragement makes great sense in pretribulationism. After all, the church will be removed from the earth before any part of the tribulation period begins. But it does not make good sense in posttribulationism.

BABIES AND YOUNG CHILDREN

Christians have different views on whether babies and young children will participate in the rapture. Some believe only the infants and young children of believers will be raptured. They find support from the days of Noah. They reason that infants and young children during Noah's time were not rescued from the flood, but only Noah and his family.

Others believe that all infants and young children will be raptured along with all Christians. (This is my view.) The same theological support for the idea that infants and young children who die go to heaven also supports the idea that they will be raptured. For example, in all the descriptions of hell found in the Bible, we never read of infants or little children there. Nor do we read of infants and little children standing before the great white throne judgment, which is the judgment of the wicked dead and the precursor to the lake of fire (Revelation 20:11-15).

The basis of the judgment of the lost involves deeds done while on earth (Revelation 20:11-13). Infants and young children must be exempt from this judgment because they have not reached the age at which they understand their accountability before God for their deeds (James 4:17). Jesus also said children have a special place in His kingdom and that adults must become like little children to enter

His kingdom (Matthew 18:1-14). King David certainly believed he would again be with his young son who died (2 Samuel 12:22-23).

It is not that infants and young children have no sin problem. They do. However, at the moment of death, the benefits of Christ's death are automatically applied to them, and that's why they go to heaven at death.

Since infants and young children go to heaven upon death, we can infer that infants and young children will also be raptured before the tribulation period. There is no plausible reason for insisting that infants and children should be targeted for God's wrath during the tribulation period.

A COMPOSITE VIEW OF THE RAPTURE

After consulting all the primary verses that deal with the rapture in the Bible, it is possible to construct a composite understanding of the rapture. The following 15 points—derived from *The Harvest Handbook of Bible Prophecy*[19]—are the most essential components of this composite understanding:

1. The Lord Himself will descend from His Father's house, where He is preparing a place for us (John 14:1-3; 1 Thessalonians 4:16).

2. He will come again to receive us to Himself (John 14:1-3).

3. He will resurrect those who have fallen asleep in Him (deceased believers whom we will not precede—1 Thessalonians 4:14-15).

4. The Lord will shout as He descends ("loud command," 1 Thessalonians 4:16 NIV). All this occurs in the "twinkling of an eye" (1 Corinthians 15:52).

5. We will hear the archangel's voice (1 Thessalonians 4:16).

6. We will also hear the trumpet call of God (1 Thessalonians 4:16), the last trumpet for the church. (Don't confuse this with the seventh trumpet of judgment upon the world during the Tribulation in Revelation 11:15.)

7. The dead in Christ will rise first (the corruptible ashes of their dead bodies are made incorruptible and joined together with their spirits, which Jesus brings with Him—1 Thessalonians 4:16-17).

8. Then we who remain alive will be changed (or made incorruptible by having our bodies made "immortal"—1 Corinthians 15:51, 53).

9. We will be caught up (raptured) together (1 Thessalonians 4:17).

10. We will be caught up in the clouds (where dead and living believers will have a monumental reunion—1 Thessalonians 4:17).

11. We will meet the Lord in the air (1 Thessalonians 4:17).

12. Christ will receive us to Himself and take us to the Father's house, "that where I am, there you may be also" (John 14:3).

13. "And so, we shall always be with the Lord" (1 Thessalonians 4:17).

14. At the call of Christ for believers, He will judge all things. Christians will stand before the judgment seat of Christ (Romans 14:10; 2 Corinthians 5:10), described in detail in 1 Corinthians 3:11-15. This judgment prepares Christians for...

15. The marriage of the Lamb. Before Christ returns to earth in

power and great glory, He will meet His bride, the church, and the marriage supper will take place. In the meantime, after the church is raptured, the world will suffer the unprecedented outpouring of God's wrath (Matthew 24:21).

DIALOGUING THE CHRISTIAN WAY

N o one likes being on the receiving end of character assassination. No one wants to be told that their personal theological position involves "fanatic exegesis" and "paltry reasoning," and that they prefer "any rubbish to the true and obvious explanation" of a Scripture passage.

To be honest, I am surprised that some Christians speak about other Christians who hold to a different prophetic position with harsher language than I've ever seen in the kingdom of the cults and the occult. And believe me when I tell you that I know what I'm talking about regarding the kingdom of the cults and the occult. I've written more than a dozen books on the cults—including *The Challenge of the Cults and New Religions* (Zondervan Publishers) and *Find It Quick Handbook on Cults and New Religions* (Harvest House Publishers). I also wrote the detailed article on the cults found in the ESV Study Bible. I've even written about satanism and a variety of occultic groups. But I've *never* witnessed a cultist or an occultist use such language of contempt for those who hold to a different viewpoint.

I am purposefully bringing this book to a close by briefly addressing five principles we can all keep in mind when dialoguing with others who believe differently than we do on prophetic issues. My goal with these principles is to generate more light than heat amid prophecy debates.

1. SPEAK THE TRUTH IN LOVE

It is not simply *what* we believe that is important, but *how we behave*. The apostle Paul struck the perfect balance when he exhorted the Ephesian Christians about the importance of "speaking the truth in love" (Ephesians 4:15). In the original Greek text, this is literally "*truthing* in love." If all prophecy students committed to "truthing in love" or "speaking the truth in love," how much more fruitful would their dialogues be! They will no doubt still end up disagreeing with each other on a number of prophetic issues, but the loving attitude can make all the difference toward better dialogue.

2. BE GENTLE AND RESPECTFUL

As a Christian, you are instructed to be "prepared to make a defense to anyone who asks you for a reason for the hope that is in you; yet do it with gentleness and respect" (1 Peter 3:15). Even when speaking with other Christians with whom we have significant differences on prophecy, we ought to show gentleness and respect.

"Gentleness" and "respect" are words that are rich in meaning. The word *gentleness* carries the idea of meekness and humility. There is not to be even the slightest hint of arrogance (see 1 Peter 3:4). This means we should not try to ram our ideas down the throat of someone we are speaking with. We should avoid speaking patronizingly. We should avoid condescension and a critical countenance. Let us not forget that gentle answers have a positive benefit—they "turn away wrath" (Proverbs 15:1). A gentle answer is much easier to swallow.

The word *respect* has two important nuances. On the one hand, we are to maintain reverential awe of God (see 1 Peter 1:17; 2:17; 3:2).

On the other hand, we are to show respect to the person with whom we are speaking (see Colossians 4:6).

I urge you to let the words *gentleness* and *respect* burn into your heart. No matter how strong your theological arguments may be for whatever position on prophecy you hold, they will have minimal effect on others if they are not communicated with gentleness and respect.

3. BE A GOOD LISTENER

James 1:19 instructs us: "Let every person be quick to hear, slow to speak, slow to anger." A key component in conversing with others about prophecy is to be a good listener.

Proverbs 18:13 provides this additional wisdom: "If one gives an answer before he hears, it is his folly and shame." It is foolish for people to blurt out opinions on matters that they have not taken the trouble to hear out carefully. One should listen well before speaking. Even if we know that we disagree strongly with a person on prophecy, we should nevertheless listen carefully to what that person says.

Listening demonstrates that you care about the person to whom you are speaking. It shows that your verbal engagement with him or her is not just a dialectic contest to see who wins an argument, but rather, it shows that they are important enough to you personally that you will give your time to hear them out. I think Norman and David Geisler are right when they say, "If people sense you are genuinely trying to understand them, they may be less defensive and let down their guard to engage in honest dialogue."[1]

4. TRY TO AVOID OFFENSE

Causing offense is one of the most potent conversation squashers on the planet. We can be 100 percent accurate about the doctrine that we share with someone, and we can be spot on in our description of a particular doctrine, but if we offend in the process of speaking, the person to whom we are speaking will likely turn away.

To illustrate, when I read that pretribs engage in "fanatic exege-sis" and have "paltry reasoning," it is hard not to be offended. Such words can be hurtful. I have personally chosen not to let such comments get to me. But the better policy would be for all believers to avoid giving such offense in the first place.

Proverbs 12:18 tells us: "There is one whose rash words are like sword thrusts, but the tongue of the wise brings healing." Thought-less words can wound people's emotions. Conversely, thoughtful words—typically spoken by wise people—bring healing to one's emotions. "Some people's normal speech pattern is constantly to accuse, belittle, manipulate, mock, insult, or condemn, and their rash words hurt other people and feel like sword thrusts. This is the opposite of the way of wisdom taught in Proverbs, for the tongue of the wise brings healing."[2]

Because words can be injurious, the psalmist requests of God: "Set a guard, O Lord, over my mouth; keep watch over the door of my lips!" (Psalm 141:3). The psalmist desired that God would provi-dentially keep him from speaking inappropriate or incautious words. He knew of the human tendency to speak wounding words to oth-ers. You and I may not necessarily intend to speak inappropriately to others, but it is certainly possible that we could do so inadvertently, thereby bringing a sudden end to our conversion. I have chosen to follow the lead of the psalmist in asking God to guard my tongue. No matter how strongly I may disagree with someone on prophecy or some other doctrine, I do not wish to injure anyone.

In James 1:26, we read some strong words: "If anyone thinks he is religious and does not bridle his tongue but deceives his heart, this person's religion is worthless." "Bridle" refers to the headgear used to control a horse, consisting of buckled straps to which a bit and reins are attached. Just as a bridle is used to control a horse, you and I must exert efforts to control our tongues. Just as a horse without restraint could gallop off in any direction, a tongue without restraint could go off in any direction and bring offense to others. We "bridle" our tongues by heeding the instructive constraints found in Scripture.

In Proverbs 15:1, we read, "A soft answer turns away wrath, but a harsh word stirs up anger." A "soft" answer is a gentle answer. One Bible scholar notes that "a gentle answer can dispel a potentially tense situation by dissolving a person's wrath. Being conciliatory in such a situation requires forethought, patience, self-control, and kindness, virtues commonly lauded in Proverbs."[3]

The phrase "harsh word" in Proverbs 15:1 means "word of pain" or "word that is hurtful." Understandably, hurtful words quickly yield anger. Nabal is an example of a man whose harsh words put David in a fighting mood (1 Samuel 25:10-13).

James 3:5-6 instructs us: "The tongue is a small part of the body, but it makes great boasts. Consider what a great forest is set on fire by a small spark. The tongue also is a fire, a world of evil among the parts of the body. It corrupts the whole body, sets the whole course of one's life on fire, and is itself set on fire by hell" (NIV). This passage reveals that though small and comparatively insignificant, "the tongue can affect great change out of all proportion to its size…The tongue has as much destructive power as a spark in a forest. It is petite but powerful."[4]

Someone said, "The tongue is but three inches long, yet it can kill a man six feet high." Never forget that the tongue can cut like a sharp razor (Psalm 52:2) and sting like a poisonous snake (Psalm 140:3). It can even kill someone (Proverbs 18:21). No one can tame the tongue (James 3:8). Thus, it is all the wiser to ask God to put a guard at our lips.

5. SHARE WORDS PEPPERED BY GRACE

In Colossians 4:6, the apostle Paul instructs us, "Let your speech always be gracious, seasoned with salt, so that you may know how you should answer everyone" (NET). I am convinced that conversing with others would be far more effective if people would make this passage the heart of their modus operandi.

Our passage tells us, "Let your speech always be gracious." The word *speech* in this verse means "word, discourse, talking." It refers to conversations the Christian has in any context. We are to be gracious toward others because God Himself is gracious to us. We ought to reflect the graciousness of God in all our encounters with people. The word "gracious" in the context of Colossians 4:6 carries the idea of "pleasing, pleasant, charming, and winsome."[5] Our conversations about prophecy ought to be brimming with such characteristics. *We can still disagree with others just as strongly*, but our verbal exchanges with people should be gracious.

The apostle Paul then tells us that our speech or conversation ought to be "seasoned with salt" (Colossians 4:6). The metaphor of salt can carry several meanings. Some suggest that since salt makes food more attractive and appealing (Matthew 5:13; Mark 9:50; Ephesians 4:29), the metaphor in Colossians may indicate that our speech is to be attractive and appealing. Others suggest that the metaphor refers to speaking in an interesting, stimulating, and wise way. Still others suggest that because salt slows spoilage, the metaphor might indicate that "our speech should be tempered so as never to be insipid, corrupt, or obscene."[6] Perhaps all these nuances of meaning have relevance in seeking to avoid prophecy wars.

Our passage closes by informing us that all of this is "so that you may know how you should answer everyone" (Colossians 4:6 NET). Such verses make it clear that it is not just *what* we say that is important, but also *how* we say it.

CONCLUSION

Our differences with our Christian brothers and sisters on the issue of prophecy are real, substantial, and important. As for me and my house, we will seek to strongly defend what we believe on prophecy, and not compromise on what we believe to be the truth. But we shall also do so in a way that honors God. We will do our best to ensure that the strength is in our *answers* and not in our *attitudes*.

BIBLIOGRAPHY

Ankerberg, John, and Dillon Burroughs. *Middle East Meltdown*. Eugene, OR: Harvest House Publishers, 2007.

Benware, Paul N. *Understanding End Times Prophecy: A Comprehensive Approach*. Chicago, IL: Moody Press, 1995.

DeMar, Gary. *End Times Fiction*. Nashville, TN: Thomas Nelson Publishers, 2001.

———. *Last Days Madness: Obsession of the Modern Church*. Atlanta, GA: American Vision, Inc., 3rd edition, 1997.

Dyer, Charles. *The Rise of Babylon: Sign of the End Times*. Chicago, IL: Moody Press, 2003.

Evidence for the Rapture: A Biblical Case for Pretribulationism, ed. John F. Hart. Chicago, IL: Moody Press, 2015.

Feinberg, Charles. *A Commentary on Revelation*. Winona Lake, IN: BMH Books, 1985.

———. *The Prophecy of Ezekiel*. Eugene, OR: Wipf and Stock Publishers, 2003.

Fruchtenbaum, Arnold. *The Footsteps of the Messiah*. San Antonio, TX: Ariel Publishing, 2004.

Hanegraaff, Hank. *The Last Disciple*. Wheaton, IL: Tyndale House Publishers, 2012.

Hindson, Ed. *Future Glory: Living in the Hope of the Rapture, Heaven, and Eternity*. Eugene, OR: Harvest Prophecy, 2021.

——. *Revelation: Unlocking the Future*. Chattanooga, TN: AMG, 2002.

Hindson, Ed, and Mark Hitchcock. *Can We Still Believe in the Rapture?* Eugene, OR: Harvest House Publishers, 2017.

Hitchcock, Mark. *55 Answers to Questions About Life After Death*. Sisters, OR: Multnomah Press, 2005.

——. *Bible Prophecy*. Wheaton, IL: Tyndale House Publishers, 1999.

——. *Could the Rapture Happen Today?* Sisters, OR: Multnomah Press, 2009.

Hitchcock, Mark, and Jeff Kinley. *Global Reset: Do Current Events Point to the Antichrist and His Worldwide Empire?* Nashville, TN: Thomas Nelson Publishers, 2022.

Hitchcock, Mark, and Thomas Ice. *The Truth Behind Left Behind*. Eugene, OR: Harvest House Publishers, 2004.

Hort, F.J.A. *The Apocalypse of St. John: I–III*. London: Macmillan Publishers, 1908.

Howe, Thomas A. *What the Bible Really Says: Breaking the Apocalypse Code*. Eugene, OR: Wipf and Stock Publishers, 2009.

Hoyt, Herman. *The End Times*. Chicago, IL: Moody Press, 1969.

Huebner, R.A. *Precious Truths Revived and Defended Through J. N. Darby*, vol. 1. Morganville, NJ: Present Truth Publishers, 1991.

Ice, Thomas, and Timothy Demy. *Prophecy Watch*. Eugene, OR: Harvest House Publishers, 1998.

———. *When the Trumpet Sounds*. Eugene, OR: Harvest House Publishers, 1995.

Ice, Thomas, and Kenneth Gentry. *The Great Tribulation: Past or Future? Two Evangelicals Debate the Question*. Grand Rapids, MI: Kregel Publications, 1999.

Ice, Thomas, and Randall Price. *Ready to Rebuild: The Imminent Plan to Rebuild the Last Days Temple*. Eugene, OR: Harvest House Publishers, 1992.

Ironside, H.A. *Revelation*. Grand Rapids, MI: Kregel Publications, 1978.

LaHaye, Tim. *A Quick Look at the Rapture and the Second Coming*. Eugene, OR: Harvest House Publishers, 2013.

———. *Revelation Illustrated and Made Plain*. Grand Rapids, MI: Zondervan Publishing House, 1975.

LaHaye, Tim, and Ed Hindson. *Global Warning: Are We on the Brink of World War III?* Eugene, OR: Harvest House Publishers, 2007.

LaHaye, Tim, and Thomas Ice. *Charting the End Times*. Eugene, OR: Harvest House Publishers, 2001.

———. *The End Times Controversy: The Second Coming Under Attack*. Eugene, OR: Harvest House Publishers, 2003.

LaHaye, Tim, and Jerry Jenkins. *Are We Living in the End Times?* Wheaton, IL: Tyndale House Publishers, 1999.

Lang, G.H. *The Revelation of Jesus Christ: Selected Studies.* Miami Springs, FL: Conley & Schoettle Publishing Co., 1985.

Miller, Steve. *Foreshadows: 12 Megaclues that Jesus' Return Is Nearer than Ever.* Eugene, OR: Harvest Prophecy, 2022.

Newell, William. *Revelation Chapter-by-Chapter.* Grand Rapids, MI: Kregel Publications, 1994.

Pache, Rene. *The Future Life.* Chicago, IL: Moody Press, 1980.

Payne, J. Barton. *The Imminent Appearing of Christ.* Grand Rapids, MI: Eerdmans Publishing Co., 1962.

Pentecost, J. Dwight. *Things to Come.* Grand Rapids, MI: Zondervan Publishing House, 1964.

Phillips, John. *Exploring Revelation.* Grand Rapids, MI: Kregel Publications, 1974.

———. *Exploring the Future: A Comprehensive Guide to Bible Prophecy.* 3rd ed. Grand Rapids, MI: Kregel Publications, 2003.

Pink, Arthur W. *The Antichrist: A Study of Satan's Christ.* Blacksburg, VA: Wilder Publishers, 2008.

Price, Randall. *Jerusalem in Prophecy.* Eugene, OR: Harvest House Publishers, 1998.

———. *Unholy War.* Eugene, OR: Harvest House Publishers, 2001.

Price, Walter K. *The Coming Antichrist.* Neptune, NJ: Loizeaux Brothers Publishers, 1985.

Reagan, David. *The Man of Lawlessness: The Antichrist in the Tribulation.* Princeton, TX: Lamb & Lion Ministries, 2012.

————. *Jesus the Lamb and the Lion*. Princeton, TX: Lamb & Lion Ministries, 2012.

Ryrie, Charles. *Come Quickly, Lord Jesus: What You Need to Know About the Rapture*. Eugene, OR: Harvest House Publishers, 1996.

————. *Dispensationalism*. Chicago, IL: Moody Press, 1965.

Showers, Renald. *Maranatha: Our Lord Come!* Bellmawr, NJ: Friends of Israel, 1995.

Stanton, Gerald. *Kept from the Hour*. Haysville, NC: Schoettle, 1991.

The Harvest Handbook of Bible Prophecy, eds. Ed Hindson and Mark Hitchcock. Eugene, OR: Harvest House Publishers, 2020.

The Popular Bible Prophecy Commentary, eds. Tim LaHaye and Ed Hindson. Eugene, OR: Harvest House Publishers, 2006.

The Popular Encyclopedia of Bible Prophecy, eds. Tim LaHaye and Ed Hindson. Eugene, OR: Harvest House Publishers, 2004.

Thomas, Robert L. *Revelation 1–7: An Exegetical Commentary*. Chicago, IL: Moody Press, 1992.

————. *Revelation 8–22: An Exegetical Commentary*. Chicago, IL: Moody Press, 1995.

Three Views on the Rapture: Pretribulation, Prewrath, or Posttribulation, ed. Stanley Gundry. Grand Rapids, MI: Zondervan Publishing House, 2010.

Walvoord, John F. *Daniel: The Key to Prophetic Revelation*. Chicago, IL: Moody Press, 1971.

————. *The Millennial Kingdom*. Grand Rapids, MI: Zondervan Publishing House, 1975.

————. *The Prophecy Knowledge Handbook.* Wheaton, IL: Victor Books, 1990.

————. *The Rapture Question.* Grand Rapids, MI: Zondervan Publishing House, 1979.

Walvoord, John F. and John E. Walvoord. *Armageddon, Oil, and the Middle East Crisis.* Grand Rapids, IL: Zondervan Publishing House, 1975.

Weremchuk, Max S. *John Nelson Darby: A Biography.* Neptune, NJ: Loizeaux Brothers, 1992.

Woods, Andy. *The Falling Away: Spiritual Departure or Physical Rapture?* Taos, NM: Dispensational Publishing House, 2018.

SCRIPTURE COPYRIGHT NOTIFICATIONS

NOTES

CHAPTER 1—BIBLE PROPHECY UNDER FIRE

1. Jon Courson, *Jon Courson's Application Commentary*, in The Bible Study App, OliveTree Bible Software.

CHAPTER 2—THE PRETRIBULATIONAL RAPTURE IN THE CROSSHAIRS

1. Ed Hindson, *Future Glory: Living in the Hope of the Rapture, Heaven, and Eternity* (Eugene, OR: Harvest House Publishers), 27-28, Kindle edition.

2. Charles Ryrie, *Come Quickly, Lord Jesus* (Eugene, OR: Harvest House Publishers, 1996), 66.

3. Mark Hitchcock, *Could the Rapture Happen Today?* (Sisters, OR: Multnomah Publishers, 2005), Apple Books edition.

CHAPTER 3—TARGETING PRETRIBULATIONAL CHRISTIANS

1. See Charles C. Ryrie, *Dispensationalism* (Chicago, IL: Moody Press, 1965), chapter 1, Kindle edition.

2. See John F. Walvoord, *The Rapture Question* (Grand Rapids, MI: Zondervan Publishers, 1979), Kindle edition.

3. Walvoord, *The Rapture Question*, Kindle edition.

4. J.C. Ryle, *Holiness* (Moscow, ID: Charles Nolan, 2001), xxiii.

5. Ryle, *Holiness*, xv.

6. Walvoord, *The Rapture Question*, Kindle edition.

7. C.S. Lewis, *Mere Christianity* (San Francisco, CA: HarperOne, 2015), 134.

8. J.I. Packer, ed. *Alive to God: Studies in Spirituality* (Downers Grove, IL: InterVarsity, 1992), 162.

9. Packer, *Alive to God*, 171.

10. Packer, *Alive to God*, 171.

11. Mark Hitchcock, *The End: A Complete Overview of Bible Prophecy and the End Times* (Carol Stream, IL: Tyndale House Publishers, 2012), Apple Books.

12. Ron Rhodes, "Millennial Madness," *Christian Research Journal*, Fall 1990, 39.

13. A 2016 poll commissioned through LifeWay Research asked 1,000 senior pastors, ministers, and priests their end times views. Pretribulationism was held by more Christian leaders than any other view. As summarized by Billy Hallowell: "Overall, 36 percent of pastors—the largest proportion by far—aligned themselves with the pretribulation view, with the second largest proportion (25 percent) saying that 'the concept of the rapture is not to be taken literally.' An additional 18 percent aligned themselves with the posttribulation belief that the rapture and the second coming of Christ are essentially one and the same." Billy Hallowell, "Is the Rapture Really Biblical? Pastors Reveal Exactly Where They Stand on Revelation, Eschatology and 'Left Behind' Theology," *The Blaze*, May 3, 2016.

CHAPTER 4—OUT WITH ISRAEL, IN WITH THE CHURCH

1. Paul N. Benware, *Understanding End Times Prophecy: A Comprehensive Approach* (Chicago, IL: Moody Press, 1995), Apple Books.

2. S. Lewis Johnson, "Paul and 'The Israel of God': An Exegetical and Eschatological Case Study," in *Essays in Honor of J. Dwight Pentecost*, eds. Stanley Toussaint and Charles Dyer (Chicago, IL: Moody Press, 1986), 189.

3. Benware, *Understanding End Times Prophecy*, Apple Books.

4. William MacDonald, *Believer's Bible Commentary*, ed. Art Farstad (Nashville, TN: Thomas Nelson Publishers, 2016), The Bible Study App.

5. Thomas Constable, "Notes on Galatians," *Constable's Expository Notes on the Bible*, www.sonic light.com/constable/notes/pdf/galatians.pdf.

6. Constable, "Notes on Galatians."

7. F.F. Bruce, *The Epistle to the Galatians* (Grand Rapids, MI: Eerdmans Publishers, 1982), 275.

8. Thomas Ice, cited in Mark Hitchcock, *The Late Great United States* (Colorado Springs, CO: Multnomah Publishers, 2009), 129-30.

CHAPTER 5—EXAMINING THE PRETERIST CASE FOR AN EARLY DATE OF REVELATION

1. Thomas D. Ice, "Has Bible Prophecy Already Been Fulfilled?," *Conservative Theological Journal*, 04:13 (Dec 2000), Galaxie Software Electronic Publishing.

2. Mark L. Hitchcock, "A Critique of the Preterist View of 'Soon' and 'Near' in Revelation," *Bibliotheca Sacra*, 163:652 (Oct 2006), Galaxie Software Electronic Publishing.

3. Norman Geisler, "A Response to Steve Gregg's Defense of Hank Hanegraaff's Partial Preterism," posted at the Norman Geisler website, http://normgeisler.com/a-response-to-steve-gregg-partial-preterism/.

4. Kenneth L. Gentry, "The Days of Vengeance: A Review Article," *The Counsel of Chalcedon*, vol. IX, no. 4., 11, insert added for clarification.

5. Kenneth L. Gentry, "The Date and Theme of Revelation," *The Counsel of Chalcedon*, vol. XV, nos. 5 & 6, 21-22.

6. Ice, "Has Bible Prophecy Already Been Fulfilled?"

7. Paul Benware and Charles C. Ryrie, *Understanding End Times Prophecy* (Chicago, IL: Moody Press, 2006), Kindle edition.

8. Benware and Ryrie, *Understanding End Times Prophecy*, Kindle edition.

9. Tim LaHaye and Thomas Ice, *The End Times Controversy: The Second Coming Under Attack* (Eugene, OR: Harvest House Publishers, 2003), 141.

10. LaHaye and Ice, *The End Times Controversy*, 7.

11. LaHaye and Ice, *The End Times Controversy*, 39.

12. Irenaeus, *Against Heresies* (Veritatis Splendor Publications, 2012), v.xxx.3, emphasis added.

13. Benware and Ryrie, *Understanding End Times Prophecy*, Kindle edition, emphasis added.

14. LaHaye and Ice, *The End Times Controversy*, 129.

15. Victorinus, *A Commentary on the Apocalypse of The Blessed John* (Great Plains Press, 2012), 10:11.

16. Eusebius, *The History of the Church*, translated by G.A. Williamson (New York: Penguin, 1989), 80-81.

17. LaHaye and Ice, *The End Times Controversy* 135, insert added for clarification.

18. R.H. Charles, cited in LaHaye and Ice, *The End Times Controversy*, 139.

19. Hitchcock, "A Critique of the Preterist View of 'Soon' and 'Near' in Revelation."

20. Kenneth Gentry, *Before Jerusalem Fell* (Chesnee, SC: Victorious Hope Publishing, 2017), 23.

21. Benware and Ryrie, *Understanding End Times Prophecy*, Kindle edition.

22. Mark L. Hitchcock, "A Critique of the Preterist View of Revelation 13 and Nero," *Bibliotheca Sacra*, 164:655 (Jul 2007), Galaxie Software Electronic Publishing.

23. LaHaye and Ice, *The End Times Controversy*, 142-43.

24. Hitchcock, "A Critique of the Preterist View of Revelation 13 and Nero."

CHAPTER 6—EXAMINING THE PRETERIST CASE FOR THE "SOON" FULFILLMENT OF PROPHECY

1. Hank Hanegraaff, *The Last Disciple* (Wheaton, IL: Tyndale House Publishers, 2012), 395.

2. Hanegraaff, *The Last Disciple*, 4.

3. Kenneth Gentry, *Before Jerusalem Fell* (Chesnee, SC: Victorious Hope Publishing, 2017), 133.

4. Thomas D. Ice, "Has Bible Prophecy Already Been Fulfilled?," *Conservative Theological Journal*, 04:13 (Dec 2000), Galaxie Software Electronic Publishing.

5. Justin Martyr, *Dialogue with Trypho* (Fig, 2012), chapter 110.

6. See Greg L. Bahnsen and Kenneth L. Gentry, *House Divided* (Institute for Christian Economics, 1997), 283. Thomas Ice and Kenneth L. Gentry, *The Great Tribulation, Past or Future? Two Evangelicals Debate the Question* (Grand Rapids, MI: Kregel Publications, 1999), 160.

7. Oecumenius, cited in *Ancient Christian Commentary*, e-Sword, Rick Meyers, 2022, insert added for clarification.

8. Albert Barnes, *Barnes' Notes on the Bible* (Grand Rapids, MI: Kregel Publishers, 1962), cited in e-Sword, Rick Meyers, 2022.

9. William F. Arndt and F. Wilbur Gingrich, *Greek-English Lexicon of the New Testament* (Chicago, IL: University of Chicago Press, 1957), 814.

10. Joseph Thayer, *Greek-English Lexicon of the New Testament* (Grand Rapids, MI: Zondervan Publishers, 1963), 616.

11. W.E. Vine, *Expository Dictionary of New Testament Words* (Nashville, TN: Thomas Nelson Publishers, 1985), 913.

12. G.H. Lang, *The Revelation of Jesus Christ: Selected Studies* (Miami Springs, FL: Conley & Schoettle Publishing Co., 1945, 1985), 387–88.

13. Tim LaHaye and Thomas Ice, *The End Times Controversy: The Second Coming Under Attack* (Eugene, OR: Harvest House Publishers, 2003), 295.

14. F. Blass and A. Debrunner, *A Greek Grammar of the New Testament and Other Early Christian Literature*, translated and revised by Robert W. Funk (Chicago, IL: The University of Chicago Press, 1961), 55–57.

15. Ice, "Has Bible Prophecy Already Been Fulfilled?"

16. LaHaye and Ice, *The End Times Controversy*, 295.

17. Norman L. Geisler, "A Friendly Response to Hank Hanegraaff's Book, *The Last Disciple*," posted at Norman Geisler website, http://normangeisler.com/response-to-hanegraaffs-last-disciple/.

18. Mark L. Hitchcock, "A Critique of the Preterist View of 'Soon' and 'Near' in Revelation," *Bibliotheca Sacra*, 163:652 (Oct 2006), Galaxie Software Electronic Publishing.

19. *The Moody Bible Commentary*, ed. Michael Rydelnik (Chicago, IL: Moody Press, 2014), in the Bible Study App, OliveTree Bible Software.

20. This view obviously conflicts with Albert Barnes's view that "soon" might refer to the initial events in Revelation, and that a long train of other prophetic events might transpire later.

21. Hitchcock, "A Critique of the Preterist View of 'Soon' and 'Near' in Revelation."

22. Wayne Grudem, *Systematic Theology*, 2nd edition (Grand Rapids, MI: Zondervan Academic, 2020), Kindle edition.

23. Kenneth Gentry, "A Preterist View of Revelation," in *Four Views on the Book of Revelation*, eds. S.N. Gundry and C.M. Pate (Grand Rapids, MI: Zondervan Publishers, 1998), 43.

24. Thomas Ice and Kenneth L. Gentry, *The Great Tribulation, Past or Future?*, 26–27.

25. R.C. Sproul, *The Last Days According to Jesus* (Grand Rapids, MI: Baker Books, 2015), 158.

26. Gary DeMar, *Last Days Madness: Obsession of the Modern Church* (Atlanta, GA: American Vision, 1997), 73.

27. Darrell L. Bock, *Luke 9:51–24:53* (Grand Rapids, MI: Baker Books, 1996), 1691-92.

28. LaHaye and Ice, *The End Times Controversy*, 121.

29. Kenneth Gentry, "A Preterist View of Revelation."

30. Richard L. Mayhue, "Jesus: A Preterist or a Futurist?" *Masters Seminary Journal*, MSJ 14:1 (Spring 2003), 9.

CHAPTER 7—EXAMINING THE PRETERIST CASE FOR AN AD 70 FULFILLMENT OF PROPHECY

1. Andrew M. Woods, "Have the Prophecies in Revelation 17–18 About Babylon Been Fulfilled? Part 1," *Bibliotheca Sacra* (January-March 2012), 79-80.

2. Woods, "Have the Prophecies in Revelation 17–18 About Babylon Been Fulfilled? Part 1," 79-80.

3. Kenneth Gentry, *Before Jerusalem Fell* (Chesnee, SC: Victorious Hope Publishing, 2017), 253.

4. Gentry, *Before Jerusalem Fell*, 250.

5. Mark L. Hitchcock, "A Critique of the Preterist View of Revelation and the Jewish War," *Bibliotheca Sacra*, 164:653 (Jan 2007), Galaxie Software Electronic Publishing.

6. Gentry, *Before Jerusalem Fell*, 248.

7. Gentry, *Before Jerusalem Fell*, 247.

8. Hitchcock, "A Critique of the Preterist View of Revelation and the Jewish War."

9. Hitchcock, "A Critique of the Preterist View of Revelation and the Jewish War."

10. Hitchcock, "A Critique of the Preterist View of Revelation and the Jewish War."

11. Kenneth L. Gentry, *He Shall Have Dominion* (Tyler, TX: Institute for Christian Economics, 1992), 412.

12. Kenneth Gentry, cited in Thomas D. Ice, "Has Bible Prophecy Already Been Fulfilled?" *Conservative Theological Journal*, 04:13 (Dec 2000), Galaxie Software Electronic Publishing.

13. Gentry, *He Shall Have Dominion*, 274.

14. Wayne Grudem, *Systematic Theology*, 2nd edition (Grand Rapids, MI: Zondervan Academic, 2020), Kindle edition, 2609.

15. Thomas Ice and Kenneth Gentry, *The Great Tribulation: Past or Future?* (Grand Rapids, MI: Kregel Publishers, 1999), 60.

16. *Let God Be True* (Brooklyn, NY: Watchtower Bible and Tract Society, 1946), 198.

17. Ice and Gentry, *The Great Tribulation: Past or Future?*, 53-54.

18. Paul Benware and Charles C. Ryrie, *Understanding End Times Prophecy* (Chicago, IL: Moody Publishers, 2006), Kindle edition.

19. John F. Walvoord, *Revelation* (Chicago, IL: Moody Press, 1980), 39.

20. Philip Edgcumbe Hughes, *The Book of the Revelation* (Grand Rapids, MI: Eerdmans Publishers, 1990), 20-21.

21. J.H. Thayer, *A Greek-English Lexicon of the New Testament* (Grand Rapids, MI: Zondervan Publishers, 1963), 490.

22. *Vine's Expository Dictionary of Biblical Words*, eds. W.E. Vine, Merrill F. Unger, and William White (Nashville, TN: Thomas Nelson Publishers, 1985), 32.

23. William F. Arndt and F. Wilbur Gingrich, *A Greek-English Lexicon of the New Testament and Other Early Christian Literature* (Chicago, IL: University of Chicago Press, 1957), 581.

24. Thayer, *A Greek-English Lexicon of the New Testament*, 451.

25. *Vine's Expository Dictionary of Biblical Words*, 556.

26. Wayne Grudem, *Systematic Theology*, 2609.

CHAPTER 8—EXAMINING THE PRETERIST CASE AGAINST PRETRIBULATIONISM

1. Hank Hanegraaff, *The Last Disciple* (Wheaton, IL: Tyndale House Publishers, 2012), 395.

2. Norman L. Geisler, "A Friendly Response to Hank Hanegraaff's Book, *The Last Disciple*," posted at Norman Geisler website, http://normangeisler.com/response-to-hanegraaffs-last-disciple/.

3. Thomas Ice, "Has Bible Prophecy Already Been Fulfilled?," Part 2, *Conservative Theological Journal*, Galaxie Software Electronic Publishing, insert added for clarification.

4. Paul Benware and Charles C. Ryrie, *Understanding End Times Prophecy* (Chicago, IL: Moody Press, 2006), Kindle edition.

5. Thomas Ice and Kenneth Gentry, *The Great Tribulation: Past or Future?* (Grand Rapids, MI: Kregel Publishers, 1999), 55.

6. E.R. Craven, cited in Tim LaHaye and Thomas Ice, *The End Times Controversy: The Second Coming Under Attack* (Eugene, OR: Harvest House Publishers, 2003), 68.

7. Gary DeMar, "There May Be Hope for Some End-Time Prophecy Theorists," American Vision (April 23, 2012), http://americanvision.org/5715/there-may-be-hope-for-some-end-time-prophecy-theorists/.

8. Renald Showers, *Maranatha: Our Lord Come!* (Bellmawr, NJ: Friends of Israel, 1995), 214.

9. Arnold Fruchtenbaum, *The Footsteps of the Messiah* (San Antonio, TX: Ariel Ministries, 2003), n.p.

10. J. Dwight Pentecost, *Things to Come: A Study in Biblical Eschatology* (Grand Rapids, MI: Zondervan, 1958), 197.

11. Mark Hitchcock and Ed Hindson, *Can We Still Believe in the Rapture?* (Eugene, OR: Harvest House Publishers, 2018), Kindle edition.

12. Arnold Fruchtenbaum, *The Footsteps of the Messiah* (San Antonio, TX: Ariel Ministries, 2020), 152.

13. Thomas R. Edgar, "An Exegesis of Rapture Passages," in *Issues in Dispensationalism*, eds. Wesley R. Willis, John R. Master, and Charles C. Ryrie (Chicago, IL: Moody Publishers, 1994), 206-7.

14. *The Bible Knowledge Commentary*, in The Bible Study App, OliveTree Bible Software.

15. DeMar, "There May Be Hope."

16. Ron Rhodes, "The Trinity: A Case Study in Implicit Truth," *Christian Research Journal*, volume 29, number 1 (2006), posted at https://www.equip.org/articles/the-trinity-a-case-study-in-implicit-truth/.

17. Gary DeMar, "A Review of the Remnant," in Thomas Ice, "Gary DeMar's End Times Fiction," article posted at Pre-Trib Research Center, https://www.pre-trib.org/dr-thomas-ice/message/gary-demar-s-end-times-fiction.

18. Ice, "Gary DeMar's End Times Fiction."

19. Ice, "Gary DeMar's End Times Fiction."

20. Fruchtenbaum, *The Footsteps of the Messiah*, 125-26.

21. Ice, "Gary DeMar's End Times Fiction."

22. *Soncino Books of the Bible*, ed. A. Cohen, 14 vols. (London: The Soncino Press, 1948), vol. 14, 325; in Ice, "Gary DeMar's End Times Fiction."

23. Ice, "Gary DeMar's End Times Fiction."

24. DeMar, "There May Be Hope."

CHAPTER 9—CHURCH HISTORY: FRIEND OR FOE OF PRETRIBULATIONISM

1. Robert Cameron, *Scriptural Truth About the Lord's Return*, 72-73, in J. Dwight Pentecost, *Things to Come* (Grand Rapids, MI: Zondervan Publishers, 1965), 272.

2. Irenaeus, cited in William Watson, "The Rapture, Antichrist, and Rebirth of Israel in Medieval Manuscripts," article posted at the Pretrib Research Center, https://www.pre-trib.org/dr-robert-thomas/message/the-rapture-antichrist-and-rebirth-of-israel-in-medieval-manuscripts/read.

3. *The Shepherd of Hermas* (CrossReach Publications, 2014), 1.4.2.

4. Francis X. Gumerlock, "The Rapture in the Apocalypse of Elijah," *Bibliotheca Sacra* (October-December, 2013), 422.

5. Lee Brainard, "Recent Pre-Trib Rapture Findings in the Early Church," article posted at the Pretrib Research Center, https://www.pre-trib.org/dr-robert-thomas/message/prophecy-in-deuteronomy/read.

6. Ephraem of Nisibis, cited in *The Harvest Handbook of Bible Prophecy*, eds. Ed Hindson, Mark Hitchcock, and Tim LaHaye (Eugene, OR: Harvest House Publishers, 2020), Kindle edition.

7. Mark Hitchcock and Ed Hindson, *Can We Still Believe in the Rapture?* (Eugene, OR: Harvest House Publishers, 2018), Kindle edition.

8. Caesarius of Arles, cited in William C. Watson, "The Antichrist, Rebirth of Israel, and Rapture in the Fathers and Medieval Manuscripts," article posted at the Pretrib Research Center, https://www.pre-trib.org/pretribfiles/pdfs/Watson-TheAntichristRebirthOfIsraelAndRaptureInTheFathers.pdf.

9. Aspringius of Beja, cited in William C. Watson, "The Antichrist, Rebirth of Israel, and Rapture in the Fathers and Medieval Manuscripts," articled cited at the Pretrib Research Center, https://www.pre-trib.org/pretribfiles/pdfs/Watson-TheAntichristRebirthOfIsraelAndRaptureInTheFathers.pdf.

10. William Watson, *Dispensationalism Before Darby* (Silverton, OR: Lampion House Publishing, 2015), 141-142. Cf. Ephraim Huit, *The Whole Prophecy of Daniel Explained* (London: 1643), 196-99.

11. Hitchcock and Hindson, *Can We Still Believe in the Rapture?*, Kindle edition.

12. Watson, *Dispensationalism Before Darby*, 138-40.

13. *The Harvest Handbook of Bible Prophecy*, Kindle edition.

14. Thomas Ice and Timothy Demy, *When the Trumpet Sounds* (Eugene, OR: Harvest House Publishers, 1995), 119.

15. Ice and Demy, *When the Trumpet Sounds*, 121.

16. Paul N. Benware, *Understanding End Times Prophecy: A Comprehensive Approach* (Chicago, IL: Moody Press, 1995), 197-98.

17. Francis X. Gumerlock, "The Rapture in the Apocalypse of Elijah," *Bibliotheca Sacra* (October-December, 2013), 418-31.

18. Thomas Ice, "A History of the Rapture Teaching," in *Popular Handbook on the Rapture*, eds. Tim LaHaye, Thomas Ice, and Ed Hindson (Eugene, OR: Harvest House Publishers, 2011), 59.

19. Mark Hitchcock, *Could the Rapture Happen Today?* (Sisters, OR: Multnomah, 2005), Apple Books edition.

20. *The Harvest Handbook of Bible Prophecy*, Kindle edition.

21. John F. Walvoord, *The Rapture Question* (Grand Rapids, MI: Zondervan Publishers, 1979), Kindle edition.

22. J. Dwight Pentecost, *Things to Come*, Apple Books.

23. Charles C. Ryrie, *Dispensationalism* (Chicago, IL: Moody Publishers, 2007), Kindle edition.

24. Thomas A. Howe, *What the Bible Really Says* (Eugene, OR: Wipf and Stock, 2009), 15.

25. Charles Ryrie, *Come Quickly, Lord Jesus* (Eugene, OR: Harvest House Publishers, 1996), 76.

26. Pentecost, *Things to Come*, Apple Books.

27. John Calvin, "Prefatory Address to King Francis," in *Institutes of the Christian Religion* (London: Wolfe & Harison, 1561), 4, cited in Ryrie, *Dispensationalism*.

28. Thomas Ice, "Myths of the Origin of Pretribulationism"—Part 2, article posted at the Pretrib Research Center, https://www.pre-trib.org/articles/all-articles/message/myths-of-the-origin-of-pretribulationism-part-2.

29. Paul R. Wilkinson, *Understanding Christian Zionism* (Bend, OR: Berean Call, 2013), Kindle edition.

30. Marvin J. Rosenthal, "Is the Church in Matthew Chapter 24?" *Zion's Fire* (Nov-Dec 1994), 10.

31. Rosenthal, "Is the Church in Matthew Chapter 24?," 10.

32. Thomas Ice, "Myths of the Origin of Pretribulationism"—Part 2, article posted at the Pretrib Research Center, https://www.pre-trib.org/articles/all-articles/message/myths-of-the-origin-of-pretribulationism-part-2.

33. Ice, "Myths of the Origin of Pretribulationism"—Part 2.

34. Ice, "Myths of the Origin of Pretribulationism"—Part 2.

35. Ice, "Myths of the Origin of Pretribulationism"—Part 2.

36. Paul R. Wilkinson, "'Left Behind or Led Astray?'—Exposed," article posted at the Pretrib Research Center, https://www.pre-trib.org/media/k2/assets/Documents/Rebuttal-statement-Left-Behind-or-Led-Astray.pdf

37. Wilkinson, "'Left Behind or Led Astray?'—Exposed."

38. William Kelly, *The Rapture of the Saints: Who Suggested It, or Rather on What Scripture?* (London: T. Weston, 1903), 12.

39. Rosenthal, "Is the Church in Matthew Chapter 24?," 10.

40. "Left Behind or Led Astray: Examining the Origins of the Secret Pre-Tribulation Rapture," Good Fight Ministries; quoted in Paul R. Wilkinson, "'Left Behind or Led Astray?'—Exposed," article posted at the Pretrib Research Center website: https://www.pre-trib.org/media/k2/assets/Documents/Rebuttal-statement-Left-Behind-or-Led-Astray.pdf.

41. Wilkinson, *Understanding Christian Zionism*, Kindle edition.

42. Wilkinson, *Understanding Christian Zionism*, Kindle edition.

43. *The Harvest Handbook of Bible Prophecy*, Kindle edition.

44. J. Barton Payne, *The Imminent Appearing of Christ* (Grand Rapids, MI: Eerdmans Publishers, 1962), 102.

45. Walvoord, *The Rapture Question*, Kindle edition.

46. Walvoord, *The Rapture Question*, Kindle edition.

47. Hitchcock and Hindson, *Can We Still Believe in the Rapture?*, Kindle edition.

CHAPTER 10—ALTERNATIVE VIEWS OF THE RAPTURE—PART 1

1. George Eldon Ladd, *The Blessed Hope* (Grand Rapids, MI: Eerdmans Publishing Co., 1956), 85-86.

2. Charles C Ryrie, *Basic Theology* (Chicago, IL: Moody Publishers, 1999), in Logos Bible Software.

3. John F. Walvoord, *The Rapture Question* (Grand Rapids, MI: Zondervan, 1979), 206, Kindle edition.

4. William MacDonald, *Believer's Bible Commentary*, ed. Art Farstad (Nashville, TN: Thomas Nelson Publishers, 2016), The Bible Study App.

5. Arnold Fruchtenbaum, *The Footsteps of the Messiah* (San Antonio, TX: Ariel Ministries, 2020), 144-45, insert added.

6. Charles C. Ryrie, *Come Quickly, Lord Jesus* (Eugene, OR: Harvest House Publishers, 1996), 97, in Mark Hitchcock and Ed Hindson, *Can We Still Believe in the Rapture?* (Eugene, OR: Harvest House Publishers, 2017), Apple Books edition.

7. Ryrie, *Basic Theology*, in Logos Bible Software.

CHAPTER 11—ALTERNATIVE VIEWS OF THE RAPTURE—PART 2

1. Norman Geisler, *Church / Last Things*, vol. 4 of *Systematic Theology* (Minneapolis, MN: Bethany House Publishers, 2005), Logos Bible Software.

2. Thomas Waugh, *When Jesus Comes* (London: Charles H. Kelly, 1901), 108.

3. Ira E. David, "Translation: When Does It Occur?" *The Dawn* (November 15, 1935), 258.

4. J. Dwight Pentecost, *Things to Come*, Apple Books.

5. Herman Hoyt, *The End Times* (Chicago, IL: Moody Press, 1969), 81, insert added for clarification.

6. *The Popular Encyclopedia of Bible Prophecy*, eds. Tim LaHaye and Ed Hindson (Eugene, OR: Harvest House Publishers, 2004), 261.

CHAPTER 12—THE BIBLICAL CASE FOR THE PRETRIBULATIONAL RAPTURE

1. Thomas Ice and Timothy Demy, *When the Trumpet Sounds* (Eugene, OR: Harvest House Publishers, 1995), 158.

2. Ed Hindson, *Future Glory: Living in the Hope of the Rapture, Heaven, and Eternity* (Eugene, OR: Harvest Prophecy, 2021), Kindle edition.

3. Renald Showers, *Maranatha: Our Lord Come!* (Bellmawr, NJ: Friends of Israel, 1995), 214.

4. Gerald Stanton, *Kept from the Hour* (Haysville, NC: Schoettle, 1991), 50.

5. John F. Walvoord, *The Rapture Question* (Grand Rapids, MI: Zondervan Publishers, 1979), 12.

6. Walvoord, *The Rapture Question*, 12.

7. Arnold Fruchtenbaum, *The Footsteps of the Messiah* (San Antonio, TX: Ariel Publishing, 2004), Logos Bible Software.

8. Marvin Vincent, cited in Showers, *Maranatha: Our Lord Come!*, 197.

9. D. Edmond Hiebert, *1 and 2 Thessalonians*, rev. ed. (Chicago: Moody, 1992), 75.

10. E. Schuyler English, *Re-Thinking the Rapture* (Travelers Rest, SC: Southern Bible, 1954), 66.

11. English, *Re-Thinking the Rapture*, 66.

12. Walvoord, *The Rapture Question*, 268.

13. Ed Hindson, *Future Glory: Living in the Hope of the Rapture, Heaven, and Eternity* (Eugene, OR: Harvest House Publishers, 2021), 27-28.

14. Mark Hitchcock and Ed Hindson, *Can We Still Believe in the Rapture?* (Eugene, OR: Harvest House Publishers, 2017), Apple Books edition.

15. *The Harvest Handbook of Bible Prophecy*, eds. Ed Hindson, Mark Hitchcock, and Tim LaHaye (Eugene, OR: Harvest House Publishers, 2020), Apple Book edition.

16. Thomas Ice and Timothy Demy, *When the Trumpet Sounds*, 40.

17. *The Harvest Handbook of Bible Prophecy*, Apple Book edition.

18. Showers, *Maranatha: Our Lord Come!*, 197.

19. *The Harvest Handbook of Bible Prophecy*, Apple Book edition.

POSTSCRIPT: DIALOGUING THE CHRISTIAN WAY

1. Norman Geisler and David Geisler, *Conversational Evangelism* (Eugene, OR: Harvest House Publishers, 2009), 48.

2. *The ESV Study Bible* (Wheaton, IL: Crossway Publishers, 2008), see notes on Proverbs 12:18.

3. John F. Walvoord and Roy B. Zuck, eds., *The Bible Knowledge Commentary: Old Testament* (Wheaton, IL: Victor Publishers, 1985), see notes on Proverbs 15:1.

4. Thomas Constable, Notes on James, see notes on James 3:5-6. Available online at www.sonic light.com/constable/notes/pdf/james.pdf.

5. Curtis Vaughan, "Colossians," in *Ephesians Through Philemon*, vol. 11 of *The Expositor's Bible Commentary*, ed. by Frank E. Gaebelein (Grand Rapids, MI: Zondervan, 1978), see notes on Colossians 4:5-6.

6. *Ryrie Study Bible* (Chicago, IL: Moody Press, 2012), see notes on Colossians 4:5-6.

OTHER GREAT HARVEST HOUSE BOOKS BY RON RHODES

To learn more about our Harvest Prophecy resources, please visit:

www.HarvestProphecyHQ.com

HARVEST PROPHECY
An Imprint of Harvest House Publishers